Women at the Crossroads

A Woman's Perspective on the Weekly Torah Portion

Midreshet B'erot Bat Ayin:
Holistic Torah Study for Women

With blessings
Chana Bracha

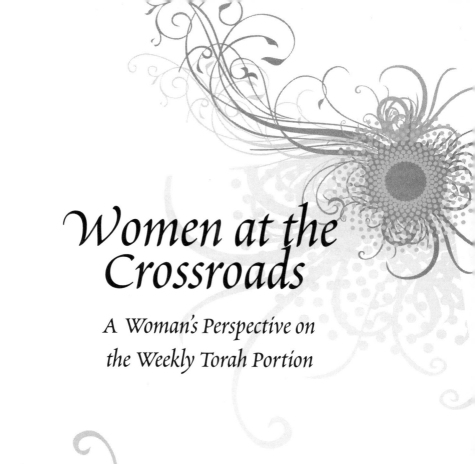

Women at the Crossroads

A Woman's Perspective on the Weekly Torah Portion

Rebbetzin Chana Bracha Siegelbaum

Midreshet B'erot Bat Ayin

Women at the Crossroads: A Woman's Perspective on the Weekly Torah Portion
Published by Midreshet B'erot Bat Ayin: Holistic Torah Study for Women

COVER DESIGN: Hila Ariel
TYPESETTING: KPS

Soft Cover ISBN: 978-1-936068-09-8

First Edition: Printed in Israel

Midreshet B'erot Bat Ayin
The Village of Bat Ayin
Gush Etzion 90913
Israel
Tel: 972.2.993.2642
Fax: 972.2.993.1215
Email: Director@berotbatayin.org

Distributed by:
Urim Publications
Penina Press
POB 52287
Jerusalem 91521, Israel
Tel: 972.2.679.7633
Fax: 972.2.679.7634
Email: urim_pub@netvision.net.il

Lambda Publishers, Inc.
527 Empire Blvd.
Brooklyn, NY 11225, USA
Tel: 718.972.5449
Fax: 781.972.6307
Email: mh@ejudaica.com

www.UrimPublications.com

Dedications

With love and devotion I dedicate this book to the loving memory of the matriarch of our family, my grandmother Trudi Erteschik of blessed memory. She passed away at the ripe age of ninety-four on the second day of Chanukah, 26 Kislev 5764 (December 21, 2003). My grandmother, *aleyha hashalom* (peace upon her) instilled in me the importance of family, gardening, homemaking, and hospitality with style. Her home was always tasteful, immaculate, and welcoming. Fruit trees, exotic plants and the most exquisite flowers blossomed in her gorgeous gardens. Even at the end of her life, she carefully tended to the flowerboxes on her patio. My grandmother taught me love and devotion for the Land of Israel. She followed my grandfather, Meir, *alav hashalom*, and made *aliyah* (immigrated) to Israel at the age of fifty-one. My grandmother was a regal woman and exuded the dignity of true Jewish femininity. She believed in the importance of education for women and encouraged my love of learning. May this book be an elevation for my grandmother's *neshamah* (soul)!

"*Mazal tov* on publishing your first book! We are sure you will be successful."

– Love Mor & Far
(Shlomo and Mirjam Vainer), Holte, Denmark

"May your first book open the hearts of women the world over, and may you have the *zechut* (merit) to continue to write many more inspiring Torah books!"

– Chava Harris, Jerusalem, Israel

In honor of Netanel Shalom's Bar Mitzvah: "We wish you a future of peace, happiness and fulfillment!"

– Grandma & Grandpa
(Jack and Noreen Siegelbaum), New Jersey, USA

"With tremendous *hakarat hatov* to Rebbetzin Siegelbaum, for showing my daughter Tziporah Sarah that creative spiritual expression and healthy living have a place in *K'lal Yisrael.*"

– Yehudit Bell, Los Angeles, USA

In honor of Shoshana Greenberg's graduation.

– Naomi Greenberg, Long Island, USA

"*Mazal tov* on the 105th birthday of cousin Regina Ruth Erteschik!"

– Naomi Greenberg

"May my beautiful sister Rifkah Leah bas Chaya Devorah be blessed soon with her *zivug hagun*!"

– Anonymous

בס"ד

Rabbi Eliezer Raphael (Lazer) Brody

Author of Pi HaBe'er, Nafshi Tidom, The Trail to Tranquility, and other books

POB 11335

Ashdod, Israel 77112

Office +972 8 8650060 / cell. +972 54 8433381

Email lazerb@bezeqint.net

---

26 Sivan, 5769

King Solomon, the wisest of all men, teaches: "Women's wisdom builds her home" (Proverbs 14:1). *Rabbenu* Yona elaborates that a woman's special capacity of insight is an integral part of her wisdom.

With Hashem's loving grace, my eyes have been rewarded the privilege of seeing Rebbetzin Chana Bracha Siegelbaum's superb manuscript of nuances and elaborations on the weekly Torah portions. As a woman of true valor and Director of Midreshet B'erot Bat Ayin for women, Rebbetzin Siegelbaum's commentaries exemplify a deep yet comprehensible and refreshing insight on the Torah portion, with special attention to details and women-oriented aspects of the Torah that are difficult to find in similar books.

Already an acclaimed and recognized expert and authority in the field of Jewish women's education, Rebbetzin Siegelbaum's Torah commentaries show that she is no less an expert with quill and parchment in hand. Her writings overflow with *emuna*, the love of her fellow Jew, and the love of our holy Land of Israel. This wonderful book should certainly grace the bookshelf of every Jewish home.

May the Almighty help Rebbetzin Siegelbaum's wellsprings to flow forth, and may she succeed in all her endeavors, seeing gratification from her family and her students always while enjoying all the best of material and spiritual blessings with long, healthy and happy years.

In eager anticipation of *Moshiach* and the full redemption of our people and the ingathering of the exiles in our beloved homeland of *Eretz Yisrael.*

Rabbi Eliezer Raphael (Lazer) Brody
Ashdod, Land of Israel

בן ציון רבינוביץ
בלאאמו"ר זצוקללה"ה
מביאלא
רח' סורוצקין 47 ירושלים

בס"ד יום ____________

לכבוד
אחינו הנדיבים עמ"ח

הנני ממלא בקשת לב על הרבנית החשובה חנה ברכה
סיגלבאום שתחי' ע"פ מנהלת מדרשת בארות בת עין
אני מכיר באופן אישי את הרבנית הנ"ל [illegible]
ונו את עבודתה בקודש זה כמה שנים בהרבצת
תורה וקרוב בנות ונשי ישראל לתורה ומצוות
וזה שיש לה הצלחה מרובה בעבודת הקודש הנ"ל
[illegible]
[illegible]

Ben Tzion Rabinowitz
The Admor of Biala
Rh' Sorotskin 47, Jerusalem
Tamuz, 5765

To the honor of my generous brothers, sons of Israel who bestows deeds of kindness,

Behold I recommend with a full heart the important Rebbetzin Chana Bracha Siegelbaum may she live, the director of Midreshet B'erot Bat Ayin. I know the Rebbetzin personally and have been guiding her with advice etc. in her holy work for several years in her *harbatzas* Torah (disseminating of Torah) and bringing Jewish girls and women close to Torah and *mitzvos*.

Baruch Hashem she is very successful in her holy *avodah* (service) explained above. She endeavors to accept into her institution serious and stable girls who desire to come close to their Creator and to the knowledge of the Jewish religion, according to what has been received upon us from generation to generation from the giving of the Torah on Mount Sinai.

The Rebbetzin, may she live, is a G-d fearing woman, who works very hard and puts great efforts to bring Jewish women close to their Father in Heaven, through pleasant ways. Fortunate are those who merit to support her and to help her with donations to assist her in building a permanent building. Whoever gives their hand for this important building will be blessed from Heaven, and the wishes of his heart will be fulfilled for good.

With Blessing,
Ben Tzion Rabbinowitz
Rebbe of Biala

B"H

Chabad of Golden Beach
International Institute for Jewish Learning

B'H

February 2nd. 2009

To whom it may concern:

We strongly recommend Rebbetzin Chana Bracha Siegelbaum as a creative Bible teacher with emphasis on women issues following Chabad Laws. She is very inspiring and this allows you to understand easily what she teaches.

Thank you for your attention,

Rabbi Chay Amar
Chabad of Golden Beach

Rabbi Chay Amar • Spiritual Director
Marco Polo Ramada Resort • 19201 Collins Ave. • Sunny Isles Beach FL 33160
Ph:305-705-0773 • Fax:305-705-0223 • E-mail: chabadofgb@bellsouth.net

RABBI ZEV LEFF
הרב זאב לף
Rabbi of Moshav Matityahu
מרא דאתרא מושב מתתיהו
Rosh Hayeshiva Yeshiva Gedola Matisyahu
ראש הישיבה ישיבה גדולה מתתיהו
d.n. modiin 71917 ד.נ. מודיעין tel. 08-976-1138 טל' fax 08-976-5326 פקס

בס"ד

I have read the manuscript of "Women at the Crossroads: A Woman's Perspective on the Weekly Torah Portion" by Mrs. Chana Bracha Siegelbaum, and have found it fascinating and enjoyable. Although I am not acquainted with Mrs. Siegelbaum personally, she is highly recommended by Torah personalities that I know, as a fine bas Torah, who possesses true Torah knowledge and strives to disseminate it through her educational endeavors.

The authoress offers short presentations on each Sedra that convey the role of the Jewish woman from various vantage points. Her presentations are not "Feminist Agenda" or apologetics for the Torah, but rather sound Torah perspectives on this sensitive and complex issue.

She quotes an array of Torah sources that provide insight and enlightenment.

I highly recommend this book, especially to women who want to be inspired to fulfill their unique role in Klal Yisroel. May Hashem bless the authoress with life and health to be able to continue to merit Klal Yisroel with her rich talents.

Sincerely
With Torah blessings,

Rabbi Zev Leff

בס״ד

י״ז אלול תשס״ו

Chana Bracha Siegelbaum has spent many years teaching her unique and inspired classes to young and to not-so-young women, touching both their hearts and their minds.

She has now given the reading public this rare combination in a lucid, readable form that will no doubt benefit many women.

Sincerely,

צפורה הלר

Tziporah Heller.

Chana Bracha Siegelbaum has spent many years teaching her unique and inspired classes to young (and not so young) women, touching both their hearts and their minds. She has now given the reading public this rare combination in a lucid, readable form that will no doubt benefit many women.

Sincerely,
Tziporah Heller

בס"ד

קול דממה דקה

A STILL SMALL VOICE

Sivan 5769 / June 2009

Chana Bracha Siegelbaum is a loving wife, a dedicated mother, and an impassioned advocate of woman's learning. As founder and dean of Midreshet B'erot Bat Ayin, she provides women with the opportunity to not only learn with their heads, but to integrate that learning into their hearts and bodies through movement, meditation and agricultural projects.

Chana Bracha is not only the founding director of this innovative seminary; she is a scholar and creative thinker in her own right. She is widely respected as a master teacher of *parshanut*. In her book, *Women at the Crossroads,* she compiles lessons from the weekly Torah portion that especially apply to women and presents them with eloquence. The material is deceptively simple for each lesson appears as a concise nugget of information. Yet the seeds of these teachings are scattered throughout libraries of source texts. Decades of research underlie this work.

Chana Bracha is to be commended for producing a book that contributes to the evolving body of teachings that give voice to the feminine perspective.

Sarah Yehudit Schneider
Founding Director of *A Still Small Voice*

A STILL SMALL VOICE
Correspondence Teachings in Classic Jewish Wisdom
Chabad 90/16 • Jerusalem, 91141 Israel • tel: (02) 628-2988
smlvoice@netvision.net.il • www.astillsmallvoice.org/

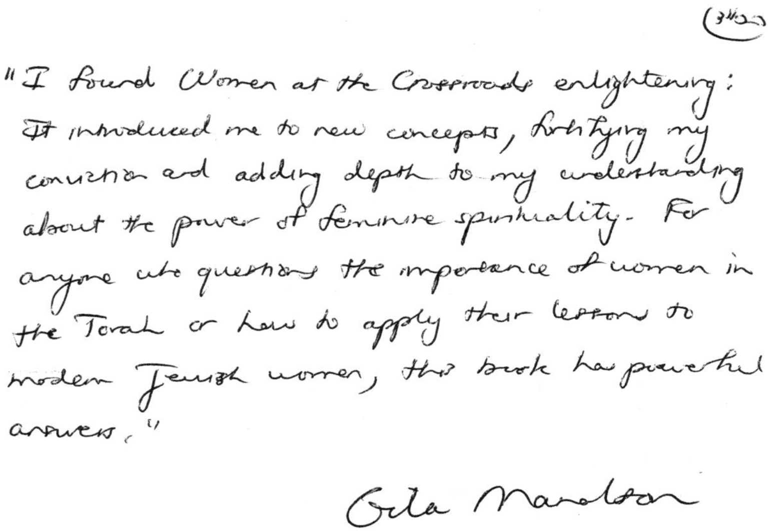
"I found Women at the Crossroads enlightening: It introduced me to new concepts, fortifying my conviction and adding depth to my understanding about the power of feminine spirituality. For anyone who questions the importance of women in the Torah or how to apply their lessons to modern Jewish women, this book has powerful answers."

Gila Manolson

I found *Women at the Crossroads* enlightening. It introduced me to new concepts, fortifying my conviction and adding depth to my understanding about the power of feminine spirituality. For anyone who questions the importance of women in the Torah or how to apply their lessons to modern Jewish women, this book has powerful answers.

Gila Manolson
(Author of *The Magic Touch*)

בס"ד

Rosh Chodesh Tammuz, 5769

Women at the Crossroads: A Woman's Perspective on the Weekly Torah Portion is very inspiring and contains a wealth of information and fascinating insights.

Chana Bracha Siegelbaum a Torah teacher of women for several decades, brings a new, powerful and thought-provoking perspective based on the Torah texts with a wide scope of commentary gleaned from Midrash, Talmud, classical, chassidic and kabbalistic commentaries.

The book offers a comprehensive in-depth analysis on women's role based on each weekly Torah portion with a unique feminine Torah perspective. Chana Bracha displays the beauty and depth of the role of women as portrayed in the Torah, and shares the joy of Jewish wife and motherhood, something that today's young women particularly need encouragement in. The underlying philosophy of laws and rituals that pertain to women are explored by examining the differences between the nature of men and women as presented in the Torah. The book extracts rich lessons from the Torah on the strength and power of women, and illustrates how the true power of women is often hidden. In fact, it is in their apparent weakness that we can see women's strength. In addition, the book demonstrates how the struggles of Biblical heroines are significant to the lives of modern women. Women from all walks of life will find in this book a refreshing perspective on women's role in religious Jewish life.

Women at the Crossroads is beautifully written, articulated in a cohesive and sensitive manner. The book offers a personal, relevant and inspirational reading for women and men as well.

I highly recommend it.

Sincerely,

Dr. Miriam Adahan

Table of Contents

PART II: THE BOOK OF SHEMOT – NAMES (EXODUS)

PART V: THE BOOK OF DEVARIM – WORDS (DEUTERONOMY)

Acknowledgements

I would like to thank my parents Drs. Shlomo and Mirjam Vainer for fostering my connection to the Land of Israel through our yearly visits during my childhood; and for sending me that ticket to Israel at a very pivotal point in my life. Thank you for believing in me, for encouraging my writing ever since childhood; and for inculcating in me that "whatever you learn, no one can take away from you."

I am grateful to my sons Mordechai Meir and Netanel Shalom for understanding the importance of my spiritual work, and making due with scrambled eggs when *Ima* (Mom) was busy at the computer. Thank you also for knowing when to insist on spending time with me and thereby helping me balance motherhood with my other callings. Your continued walk in the way of the Torah gives me much *nachat* (spiritual pleasure). Thank you to my daughter-in-law Na'amah Rachel for your receptiveness and interest in discussing women's Torah with me and for raising my granddaughters Shirah and Hodayah to love Torah and *mitzvot.*

Special thanks goes out to my parents-in-law Jack and Noreen Siegelbaum for your loving care, interest in our lives and continuous generosity.

To my dear past, present and future students of Midreshet B'erot

Bat Ayin, thank you for allowing me to teach you Torah, for your receptivity, and depth of understanding. I am inspired by your sincere yearning to bring Torah into your personal lives. Thank you for opening my mind to the many dilemmas and issues with the traditional role of Women in Judaism that face the new generation.

I appreciate the readers of my *Woman's Perspective on the Weekly Torah Portion* email over the years. Your numerous questions and comments have greatly refined many of the concepts discussed in this book.

I am forever grateful to Rabbi Mordechai Goldstein of Diaspora Yeshiva who introduced me to the Torah in 1980 and taught me devotion to the learning of Torah and to living in strict adherence with Halachah (Jewish law).

I appreciate the encouragement and blessings of the Biala Rebbe (Rabbi Ben Tzion Rabbinowitz), my spiritual guide who I turn to in times of need.

I am very grateful for the encouragement and endorsement of Rabbi Eliezer Raphael (Lazer) Brody which has greatly strengthened my self-confidence and ability to continue to write and publish with G-d's help.

I acknowledge the scholarship and friendship of Sarah Yehudit Schneider. Your eloquent and profound writings on kabbalistic concepts connected to the feminine have greatly inspired me. I treasure our telephone *chevruta* (study-partnership); thank you for being so generous with your time and for discussing my questions in the esoteric Torah realm.

My thanks and appreciation goes to my friends Shoshana Lepon, Sherri Mandell, and especially to Nama Frenkel for your encouragement and advice regarding the process of publishing this book.

To B'erot alumna Hila Ariel for your professional and artistic cover design, and for going above and beyond your job and spending many hours in research to assist us with the numerous details connected to publishing this book.

To B'erot alumna Carina Rock for your unique feminine illustrations, created with your heart and soul.

To B'erot students and alumnae Celine Aya Kraus, Gani (Jenna) Domber and Esther Edison not only for your perceptive expert editing skills, but moreover, for your constructive critique which helped improve the book.

To B'erot staff member Chava Brown for taking on the production of this project, and thereby acting as the "midwife" of my first published book.

To my personal assistant and spiritual "labor coach" Elana Roth for noticing the minute details during the editing process, and for assisting me in so many ways. Your gentle support is like a fresh breath of air facilitating my continued work.

To all the dedicated B'erot staff members, especially Elana Benarroch and Yael BenLev, who have learned to run the *midrasha* (Torah seminary for women) with less input from me, allowing me to dedicate a great part of my time to my life's passion: research and writing.

Words cannot express my great appreciation for my dear husband Dr. Mechael Chaim, who has stood by my side for almost thirty years through both rough and blessed times. Thank you for your kind support and devotion, for being such great *Abba* (Dad) to our children, allowing me to pursue my callings, while gently reminding me of my wifely duties. With great patience you taught me to write in English, making corrections on the first version of every *parashah* sheet. You are my loyal life-partner, teacher and guide, my admirer, critic and friend, always there for me when I need you, lending your emphatic listening ear and keeping my free spirit anchored to the conventional Torah way.

Thank you Hashem for blessing me with health, energy, inspiration, endurance and the ability to write and teach! May I always remain humble and recognize that everything is from You!

Introduction

With gratitude to Hashem, I'm excited to present to you *Women at the Crossroads: A Woman's Perspective on the Weekly Torah Portion*. After circulating via email for the last twelve years, these reflections have finally been compiled in a printed book version. The overwhelming amount of comments and questions, received in response to my weekly e-newsletters, confirm the unquestionable need for a feminine perspective on the Torah. Women from all walks of life are seeking an intimate connection with the Torah texts. I hope this book facilitates Jewish women in relating the Torah to the way their personal experiences, aspirations, spirituality, and relationships operate in their own lives. It can serve as a complementary sourcebook assisting teachers in preparing classes for women, or as a textbook for women's study groups. The book may also be helpful for preparing words of Torah to share at the Shabbat-table, or simply as inspirational reading for women and even men of all ages.

I first wrote *Women at the Crossroads* week by week in 5757 (1996–1997), when Hashem blessed me with our second son after more than fourteen years of secondary infertility. In the wake of the birth of Netanel Shalom, Hashem filled me with a surge of creative energy; hence in that same year I gave birth to Midreshet B'erot Bat Ayin: Holistic Torah

Study for Women. These events combined with the inspiring stories of my students became the springboard for this comprehensive analysis of women and women's issues related to each weekly Torah portion.

My personal experience juggling motherhood with these other spiritual endeavors supports the main message of both my writing and teaching at the *midrasha*, that motherhood and career go hand in hand. When we dedicate our time and energy to being a wifes and mothers, Hashem blesses us to become particularly fruitful in other areas as well. While I was busy in the creative pursuit of nurturing my infant full time, every moment of my day became loaded with creative potential. I tuned into a deeper understanding of the feminine perspective of the Torah, and was inspired to seize the time and a pen during the short time my baby was napping to express these Torah concepts in writing. My own life experience thus confirms my outlook that the highest achievements of Jewish femininity are accomplished specifically through fulfilling the traditional role of women in Judaism, rather than by attempting to imitate the more masculine Jewish rituals.

For most Jewish women, the processes of pregnancy, birth, nurturing life, and personal prayer bring us much closer to Hashem than the experience of being in the spotlight by leading prayer services or officiating as Rabbis. Although Devorah the Prophetess has been misused as a model for female rabbis, she actually attributes her main accomplishment to her role as a Jewish mother. Looking closely at the text reveals that as great as Devorah was in her capacity of prophetess, leader, and judge, she first and foremost took pride in her role as a mother, which she believed outweighed all of her other great accomplishments. We learn this from Devorah's self-proclaimed title: "…I Devorah arose, I arose a mother in Israel" (*Shoftim* 5:7). Other female role models in the Torah teach us, similarly, how specifically feminine qualities convey the greatest contribution to the molding of the Jewish people throughout the ages. They pave the way towards the long awaited world peace and harmony of our final redemption.

The process of redemption is intrinsically linked to women. It is known that not only the past redemption from Egypt took place in the merit of the righteous women (*Sotah* 11b), but also the future redemption will be in their merit (*Kav HaYashar*, Chapter 82). As Ariza"l teaches, the future redemption will follow the pattern of the Exodus (*Sha'ar HaGilgulim*, Introduction 20). Kabbalistically this is reflected in the rise of the feminine archetype from a small point of the lowest *sefirah* (Divine emanation), *malchut* (royalty), to a full stature with all ten *sefirot*, as Ariza"l explains (*Etz Chayim,* Gate 36:1). We remain in exile as long as the light of the feminine is not completely evolved and revealed in the world (Rabbi Shlomo Eliyashev, the *Leshem* on the diminished moon). On a down-to-earth level, we experience the rays of the feminine radiance unfolding through the renewed thirst among Jewish women to reclaim their traditions and heritage, and through women's Torah scholarship, and leadership in the Jewish community. In my book I introduce original Torah insights on the the importance of the more feminine attributes, such as active listening, empathy, and meditation, which only recently experienced a renaissance in the modern world. Through *tzniut* (modesty), and an emphasis on enabling the growth of others, women have the opportunity to emulate the ways of G-d, Who contracted Himself and hid His presence in order to leave room for creation.

As we draw nearer to the end of exile and darkness, the inner light of the Torah emerges and reveals a deeper truth behind what is apparent on the surface. While western society may accuse Torah of being too old fashioned or downright denigrating to the modern day woman, this very misunderstanding can become an impetus for clarifying controversial Torah laws and concepts in a deeper way. It is only the competitive western outlook on life that influences us to judge according to outer manifestations of success. With Hashem's help, this book will enable us to get in touch with the inner reality that we so often neglect in lieu of the externally projected expectations of society. When we fulfill our goal to serve Hashem to the best of our ability, the question of who is more important becomes irrelevant (see *Yalkut Shimoni, Shoftim* 4:42).

The first printed version of *Women at the Crossroads: A Woman's Perspective on the Weekly Torah Portion* is published in the honor of the Bat Mitzvah of Midreshet B'erot Bat Ayin, her twin sister, founded on *Tu B'Av*, 5757 (August 18, 1997). This unique *midrasha* is filled with spiritual Jewish women seeking to return not only to their roots but also to serious Torah study; integrating textual learning with creative expression, Chassidism, and cultivating the Land.

Here, in the heart of the Judean hills we teach the values of Women's Torah as expressed in my book. We believe that this Torah is very different and unique, reflecting the physiological differences between men and women. Rather than encourage women to learn Talmud the way men do, we give them the opportunity to spin the finest thread from the materials of *Tanach* (Bible studies), Halachah, Kabbalah, Chassidism, creativity, and gardening. Through the inner dimension of Torah, we reframe traditional women's roles in the Jewish world, empowering women to value and embrace Jewish motherhood and homemaking. Here, we raise Jewish women to embrace their Jewish femininity and let their inner light shine gently forth, together with it the radiance of the *Shechinah* (Hashem's Feminine Indwelling Presence).

Our *midrasha* has, thank G-d, become a model and benchmark for women's Torah learning. Several alumnae have told me that they realized, only later in life, how much Midreshet B'erot Bat Ayin has molded their lives. Many gifted artists and musicians have been empowered to express their talents in the sweet Torah way. Our alumnae make up a large percentage of the performing artists in the Torah world; some produced their first Torah albums in Bat Ayin. In this way B'erot has a tremendous influence on the growing women's Torah culture. The *midrasha* has made a definite impact, not only on the hundreds of students who have learned with us over the years, but even on those who visited briefly, or who connected with our vision through the teachings of this book, which has been circulated via email to several thousands from all over the world.

I envision Midreshet B'erot Bat Ayin becoming a unifying center for the Torah of our Mothers, where women the world over can nurture their *neshamot* (souls) with our Torah publications, homegrown organic produce, herbal remedies, meditative movement and healing sessions – imbuing the world with a taste of the Garden of Eden.

It is my hope and deepest prayer that my teachings of women's

Torah presented in this book will help reveal the lost light of the moon and teach Jewish women to reclaim their feminine heritage by returning to the Torah of our Mothers and to our homeland. May the accumulated light of all these holy Jewish women bring back the Feminine Indwelling Presence to the Land of Israel!

With blessings of the Torah and the Land,
Chana Bracha Siegelbaum
Sivan 5769, June 2009

director@berotbatayin.org
www.berotbatayin.org

The Book of Bereishit
The Beginning (Genesis)

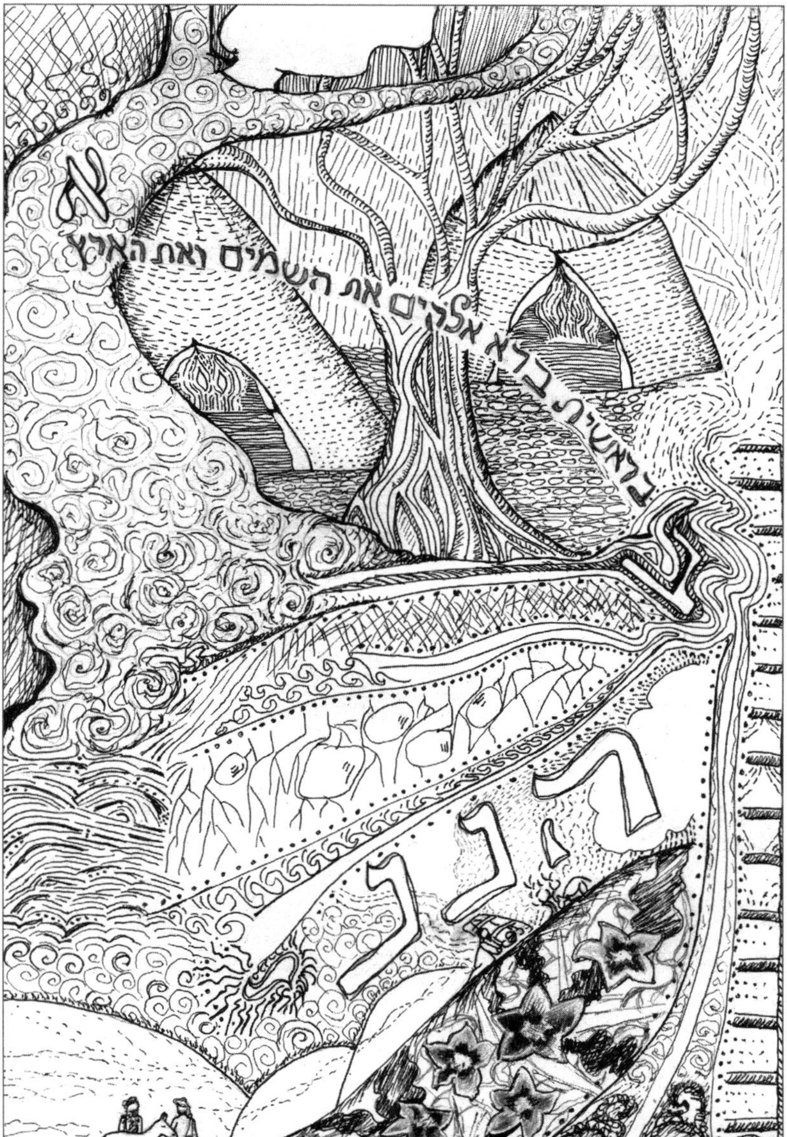

Parashat Bereishit

The Torah teaches us that man and woman were originally created as one being: "G-d created the human being in His own image, in the image of G-d He created **him**; male and female He created **them**" (*Bereishit* 1:27).

In the Image of G-d

Why does the Torah jump from the singular "him" to the plural "them" when describing the first human being? This change from singular to plural indicates the transition from the spiritual realm – where man and woman were one inseparable being – to the physical realm – where mankind is split into two different genders, each with its own unique physical and spiritual attributes. The equal status of man and woman is clear, as both are manifestations of G-d's image. G-d is One, and therefore has no higher or lower image.

An Equal Match

In *Bereishit* 2:18, woman's role is described in relation to man: "Hashem G-d said, It is not good for man to be alone, I will make a helper to match him." A man without a woman can never be complete. This fundamental principle is reflected in our oral tradition, "The man who has no wife lacks everything. He has no joy, no blessing, nothing good, no knowledge, no comfort, no peace" (*Yevamot* 62b). The woman who completes man is described in Hebrew as an *ezer kenegedo*, an expression not easily translated. The word *ezer* means helper; but the term *kenegedo* has several meanings: opposite, against, facing, contrary to, matching, parallel, and in opposition to another. The common denominator of all these expressions is equality. You can only be an opponent in chess if you are an equal player. Only a well-matched challenge can sharpen and refine the game. The reason woman perfects man in the game of life is that she is his equal match. She complements him in every way. A woman who realizes and enjoys her unique femininity is able to bring out the best in man, as King Shlomo wrote: "A virtuous woman is the crown of her husband" (*Mishlei* 12:4).

Side by Side

"Hashem G-d built the rib (*tzela*), which he had taken from the man into a woman, and He brought her unto the man" (*Bereishit* 2:22). The common understanding is that G-d created Chava from one of Adam's ribs. However, a more accurate translation reveals that she was actually created specifically from his side. Rashi explains, the word *tzela* means "of his side," similar to "and for the second **side** of the *Mishkan*" (Tabernacle) (*Shemot* 26:20). This explains the saying of our sages, "They were created with two faces" (*Eruvin* 18a). Thus, the creation of Chava involved her being divided from her other half. Her coming into being through man's side enabled their relationship to be that of equal partners, walking through life side by side.

The Building of Woman

"Hashem G-d built..." If man was originally created with two faces, it would have been sufficient to simply say that G-d separated them and closed Adam's flesh. Why did the Torah add the element of building? Rashi explains that G-d built Chava in the way most suitable to serve her purpose: "As a structure wide below and narrower above in order to receive the fetus, just as a storehouse for wheat is wide at the base and narrow at the top so that its weight should not strain the walls." *Kli Yakar* understands the word "built" to be connected with the intimacy between husband and wife, which serves to build the world. Therefore, when Sarah gave her handmaid to Avraham as a wife, she said, "...so that also I will be built (bear children) through her" (*Bereishit* 16:2).

Additional Intuition

The Hebrew word *binah* means both building and intuition. Rabbi Eliezer in the name of Rabbi Yossi son of Zimra said, "She was given more intuition than man" (*Bereishit Rabbah* 18:1). According to Rabbi Adin Steinsaltz, the woman's extra intuition endows her with the character trait of abundant curiosity. The act of eating from the Tree of Knowledge was, in a certain respect, the result of this curiosity. Although curiosity in itself is neutral, when it exceeds its boundaries it can become extremely dangerous. We elevate and redirect our curiosity to a higher purpose when we use it to help others. For example, how would we know that our neighbors are in need of help unless we inquired about their welfare? It is our challenge as women to use our Divine gift of additional intuition to stay in tune with our purpose and guide others on their path.

Within the Garden

"Hashem G-d planted a garden eastward in Eden, and there He put the man whom he had formed" (*Bereishit* 2:8). Rabbeinu Bachaya notes that man is created outside the Garden of Eden, whereas the woman is created within the Garden, where the whole separation process took place. This may explain why women exhibit greater sensitivity and yearning for harmony, as we naturally aspire to return to our inherent connection to Eden. Women pave the way for "...turning our swords into ploughshares" (*Micha* 4:3), as we rebuild the Garden of Eden bit by bit.

Parashat Noach

Just like Chava is the archetype of all women, Sarah is the prototype of all Jewish women. Sarah personifies the synthesis of being a good wife and an independent woman. "Avram and Nachor took for themselves wives: the name of Avram's wife was Sarai; and the name of Nachor's wife was Milkah, the daughter of Haran, the father of Milkah, and the father of Yiskah" (*Bereishit* 11:29).

Who is Yiskah?

The verse describing Avram's and Sarai's marriage is somewhat obscure. It is not clear who Yiskah is and why she is mentioned in this context. Rashi explains that Yiskah is Sarah; Yiskah means "to see or look," and Sarah was given this second name because she could see the future through prophecy and because everybody gazed at her beauty. In addition, the name Yiskah is from the same root as *nesichah* which means princess (sharing the letters *samech*, *chaf* and *heh*). Likewise, the name Sarah is from the same root as *serarah*, which means rulership. In our Torah portion, Sarah is called Sarai, and Avraham is called Avram. Later, the Hebrew letter *heh* is added to both of their names. (For now, we will not address the distinction between the names Sarai and Sarah).

A Ruler in Her Own Right

Be'er b'Sadeh asks why the Torah only mentions that Milkah is the daughter of Haran without mentioning that Sarai is his daughter too.

He answers that Milkah was described as Haran's daughter because she resembled him; both of their hearts were divided between worshipping idols or worshipping G-d. However, Sarai did not resemble her father in any way. Therefore, she is called Yiskah from the word *nesichut*, meaning princess and rulership. She ruled over herself and was not negatively influenced by others. Moreover, Scripture does not call Sarai the daughter of Haran but rather, it is written that Haran is the father of Yiskah. This alludes to the fact that Haran was on a lower level than Yiskah, since it is only in her merit that Scripture publicizes his name.

Sarah's Dual Nature

"Avram's wife was Sarai." The name Sarai or Sarah is often mentioned together with Avram or Avraham, respectively. The name Yiskah, however, which signifies the aspect of her prophetic spirit, is never mentioned in connection with Avraham. This is because in regards to prophecy, Sarah was independent and not influenced by anyone. She possessed a gift of prophecy superior to Avraham (see Rashi, *Bereishit* 21:12), which was inherent within her even before she married him. Since a person's name signifies her essence, Sarah's two names teach us about her dual nature. As Avraham's wife performing the will of her husband, she is called Sarah; as the prophetess who sees with prophetic spirit, she is called Yiskah.

Spiritual Independence in the Shade of her Man

Sarah is referred to both as Avraham's wife and as an independent woman, Yiskah. By mentioning both the name Sarai and Yiskah together, our verse connects the two natures of Sarah. This is the synthesis that every woman is required to make. It is our task to build up our husbands, while simultaneously retaining our own spiritual independence. Just as Hashem told Avraham to listen to Sarah, because of her more refined spirit of prophecy, so does the spiritual power of every woman compel her husband to follow her advice.

The True Jewish Princess

At her death, Sarah is not given the title "Wife of Avraham." She is simply mentioned in her own right, as the verse reads, "Sarah died in Kiriyat Arba" (*Bereishit* 23:2). When she left this world having fulfilled her life, she did not need to stand in the shadow of her husband. Her individual perfection and merit stood alone. This is Yiskah, the true Jewish princess. From her, we learn that every Jewish woman, aside from being her husband's right hand, must develop her own spiritual connection with Hashem. This level of holiness enables her to become "A woman of valor [who] is a crown to her husband" (*Mishlei* 12:4).

Parashat Lech Lecha

"Avram took Sarai his wife, and Lot his brother's son, and all their possesions that they had gathered, and the souls that they had made in Charan" (*Bereishit* 12:5). While Avraham is famous for his willingness to leave his land, birthplace, and father's house in order to follow G-d to an unknown place, the tremendous faith of his wife Sarah, who followed her husband without a word of complaint, is no less commendable.

Beside Her husband Every Step of the Way

"The home is the wife..." (*Yoma* 2a). A woman is naturally more attached to her house than her husband, because she is the queen of her home. There, she has set up her cooking quarters and living space. She knows her way to the well. The grass and flowers on her path, like the faces of her neighboring friends, make up the familiar environment that brings her security and shelter. However, Sarah's trust in Avraham and in G-d, Who had commanded her husband, was so great that it outweighed any natural attachment to her home. Without ever questioning her husband, she walked beside him every step of the way.

Her Own Spiritual Sphere

Rashi learns from *Bereishit* 12:5, "...the souls that they had made in Charan," that Sarah, together with Avraham, was involved in the spiritual work of bringing people under the wings of the *Shechinah*

(Hashem's Feminine Indwelling Presence in the world). While Avraham was busy teaching the men, a circle of women would crowd together in Sarah's tent to learn from her words of wisdom. Besides making it possible for Avraham to teach people Torah by providing them with nourishing meals, in her own sphere of spiritual work, she independently taught classes and brought countless women closer to G-d.

Modesty – A Jewish Woman's Pride

"Every woman compared to Sarah is like a monkey compared to a human being" (*Baba Batra* 58a). When the Egyptians spotted Sarah, they found her worthy to marry Pharaoh, on account of her striking beauty. "He said to Sarai his wife, Behold now I know that you are a woman of beautiful appearance" (*Bereishit* 12:11). Is it possible that Avraham was not aware of Sarah's beauty until now? Rashi explains that he had not perceived her beauty because of his – and Sarah's – extreme modesty. The relationship between Avraham and Sarah was profoundly spiritual. Avraham was only aware of her inner beauty and holiness. Its outer physical manifestation was not important to him. Likewise, Sarah did not feel self-important because of her attractiveness. Rather, her modesty compelled her to hide her intense beauty.

On Account of the Wife

After Sarah had been abducted and then released by Pharaoh because of the plagues brought about through Sarah's command (Rashi, *Bereishit* 20:18), Pharaoh sent her away with gifts for Avraham: "To Avram he did well for her sake and he had sheep and oxen" (*Bereishit* 12:16). Why would Avraham receive presents in such a shameful manner? This question is accentuated by Avraham's subsequent refusal to accept anything from the King of Sedom, whose gifts he actually deserved since he had previously saved him in war (ibid. 14:23).

Abarbanel notes that the Torah did not state, "Pharaoh gave him sheep and cattle etc." The language "he had sheep and oxen" indicates that Avraham already had these things in his possession, not that Pharaoh gave them to him now. This implies that the true giver of the oxen was Hashem, who is the subject of the next verse. In this way, the

Torah testifies to the righteousness of Sarah, for whose sake Hashem blessed Avraham. The Talmud concludes: "A man should always be careful to honor his wife, for the *bracha* (blessing) is only in his house on account of his wife, as it says, 'And to Avram he did well for her sake'" (*Baba Metzia* 59a). From here we learn that Avraham did not receive a handout from a king of flesh and blood, but rather he was accepting a blessing from Hashem – the King of kings.

The Heh Added to Avraham Derives from Sarai

In this week's *parashah*, Avram and Sarai's names were changed to Avraham and Sarah. This change is connected with their ability to have children. "Hashem said to Avram, Sarai, your wife, you shall not call her name Sarai, because Sarah is her name" (*Bereishit* 17:15). The Hebrew words for man and woman are *ish* and *isha*. The letters that distinguish them are *yud* and *heh*. *Kli Yakar* explains that Hashem exchanged the masculine *yud* of Sarai's name with the letter *heh*, in order to empower her with feminine energy and enable her to give birth. Hashem created the world with the letter *heh*. Therefore, this letter is endowed with the power of procreation (*Bereishit* 2:4, see also Rashi ad loco). The *yud* has the numerical value of ten whereas the *heh* is equal to five. Thus, the *yud* in Sarai's name equals the sum of both the *heh* with which it was exchanged and the *heh* that was added to Avram's name. The *heh* with its birthing power was added to Avram's name from the *yud* of Sarai to indicate that it was Sarah's merit that caused both of them to give birth to the progenitor of the Jewish people. Whereas Avraham was the father of many nations, Sarah alone was selected to be the mother of the Jewish people. From this we learn that Jewish descent follows the mother.

Fit to Be a Ruler of the World

Regarding the change of Avraham's name, the Torah states "...your name shall be..." (*Bereishit* 17:5). Whereas by Sarah, it simply writes, "Sarah is her name." The *Ran* explains that Avraham was not worthy of being called Avraham until after his *brit milah* (circumcision). Sarah, however, had no imperfection and was ready to be ruler over the world even before Avraham. Still, she had to wait until Avraham had perfected himself; only then could her true nature be revealed to the world. "I will bless her and also give you a son from her, and I will bless her and she shall become nations, kings of people shall be from her" (*Bereishit* 17:16). Just as Sarah followed Avraham towards an unknown destiny for the sake of G-d, so did she have an equal share in his mission as the leader of many nations, as it states: "Sarai she is Sarah. First she was a ruler to her nation and in the end she became a ruler to the whole world" (*Berachot* 17a).

Parashat Vayera

"They asked him, Where is Sarah your wife? He answered, Behold in the tent" (*Bereishit* 18:9). *Sforno* explains that the angels asked for Sarah because G-d had already imparted to Avraham the good tidings of Sarah's forthcoming pregnancy and birth. Therefore, their mission was to tell Sarah the good news, because the happiness of her anticipation would enhance the development of her fetus. This teaches us that there is an inherent connection between the emotions of the mother and her unborn child – a fact well known to our sages, which science only recently has begun to discover.

Why Did the Angels Ask for Sarah?

According to *Be'er Mayim Chayim* the angels asked for Sarah because of the importance of the wife's participation in *hachnasat orchim*, (welcoming guests). The presence of the woman makes the guests feel welcome when her gestures indicate that she is pleased with their visit. The mitzvah of welcoming guests also imparts the merit of bearing children. When we actively show our love for others by hosting and welcoming guests, it follows that we are ready to behave lovingly to the guests of our womb. Since the angels were aware of Sarah's righteousness, they expected that she would want to participate in welcoming them. They were, therefore, surprised when she was nowhere to be seen.

Behold in the Tent

Avraham answered that despite the importance of welcoming guests, "All the honor of a king's daughter is within" (*Tehillim* 45:14). This is why Sarah, out of modesty, remained in the tent. According to Rashi, the ministering angels' question was rhetorical, since as G-d's messengers they knew where Sarah was. Their question was intended to call attention to her modesty and thus endear her to her husband. Rashi adds a second explanation, the angels asked for Sarah in order to send her "the wine cup of blessing." Sarah had to partake of this cup, since it brings blessings down from above and permeates the household with holiness. Until this day, it is a mitzvah for the husband to ensure that the *kos bracha* (wine cup of blessing held during grace after meals) is sent to his wife.

Where is Her Spiritual Place?

Kli Yakar remarks that Avraham was already well aware of Sarah's modesty and did not need the angels to remind him. Their question was not directed at Sarah's physical location; rather they asked about where she was holding spiritually. The angels wanted to prevent Avraham from thinking it was Sarah's fault that they didn't have children, since the reward for modesty is to bear kings as we learn from Tamar (*Megillah* 10b). The question "Where is Sarah?" thus meant, "at what level are her deeds that she should be worthy of a son?" The answer given is "She is in the tent" – the level of her modesty makes her worthy of giving birth to holy offspring.

Royalty in the Merit of Modesty

What is the connection between modesty and conceiving children worthy of kingship? On the surface, being modest shows that we are ready to diminish our own selfhood in order to make room for someone other than ourselves. This quality is necessary to conceive extraordinarily high *neshamot* (souls), worthy of royalty. On a deeper level, Kabbalah teaches that "*malchut* (royalty) has nothing of its own" (Ariza"l, *Etz Chayim,* Gate 6:5). Among the ten *sefirot*, *malchut* is the last and "lowest," it has no unique individual characteristic other than what the remaining *sefirot* pour into it. In this way, *malchut* becomes a pure channel serving as a link to receive and manifest holiness into the world. Therefore, a Jewish king must be especially modest in order to include and unify the entire Jewish people. Bringing down such a holy soul suitable to become a Jewish king necessitates that his mother too becomes a pure channel without the barrier of the ego. Moreover, since the mother imparts her essence to her children; through perfecting the quality of modesty, she merits conceiving modest children worthy of kingdom. (See our explanation on *Parashat Emor* on page 115). It therefore makes sense, that Sarah who modestly kept her superior qualities "within the tent" without flaunting her virtues outwardly, became worthy to conceive royal seed.

Peace is Greater Than Truth

"Sarah laughed within herself, saying, After I am faded shall I have pleasure, my lord being old also? Hashem said to Avraham, Why did Sarah laugh, saying, shall I really bear, I being old?" (*Bereishit* 18:12–13) Rashi points out that G-d changed Sarah's words when addressing Avraham. Rather than quote Sarah's words – "and my lord being old," Scripture changed her words to maintain peace between them. This change is entirely justified, since nothing positive would have been gained had Hashem mentioned that Sarah was concerned about her husband being old. From here we learn that it is permitted to slightly adapt the truth for the sake of preserving peace between people, as long as it does not cause any undue harm (Rashi, *Bereishit* 18:13). Rabbi S.R. Hirsch expresses a romantic outlook on marriage: "No matter how old the husband may be, it is preferable that he doesn't know that his wife considers him old. To each other, husband and wife must forever remain youthful."

Why Did Sarah Laugh?

Ohr HaChayim notices that Avraham also laughed when Hashem promised him that he would have a son with Sarah (*Bereishit* 17:17). What is the difference between the laughter of Avraham and the laughter of Sarah? Onkelos translates Avraham's laughter as *chadei* – to rejoice – and Sarah's laughter *chayechet* – to mock. Why does Onkelos translate the same word in two completely different ways? Rabbi Mattis Weinberg explains that Avraham spoke in a general language saying, "...shall a child be born **to him** who is a hundred years old?" whereas Sarah placed herself in the center, "...after **I was** faded, **I had** pleasure?" Avraham spoke in the future tense indicating that the future might deviate from the usual way of the past. However, Sarah spoke in the past tense emphasizing that what was will continue to be, disbelieving that the nature of her body would be altered. Nonetheless, *Kli Yakar* ascribes it to her praise that she only laughed within herself, never daring to bring this laughter to her lips. Sarah was only reproved for the little laughter in her thoughts; the sin she had to refine was so subtle, so small. This only emphasizes her greatness.

Why Did Sarah Deny?

"Then Sarah denied, saying, I laughed not; for she feared. He said, No, but you did laugh" (*Bereishit* 18:15). *Ohr HaChayim* comments on the words, "for she feared," explaining that the heart of the faithful servant will be filled with fear even over an accidental transgression. Nevertheless, all the commentaries are astonished that the righteous Sarah would deny the words of G-d.

Rectified Laughter

According to *Sefat Emet*, Sarah had already repaired the sin of her laughter, erasing it by means of her immediate repentance. However, only repentance out of love and not out of fear transforms the transgression into merit. At first, Sarah had only repented out of fear, as it states, "for she feared." However, Avraham who had reached the aspect of repentance out of love, told her, "No, but you did laugh," meaning that a different quality of repentance was still necessary in order to transform the blemish of having laughed into a merit. The indication that Sarah ultimately succeeded in reaching this level of repentance is expressed in the name of Yitzchak, which means "He will laugh." When Sarah gave him this name, she happily exclaimed, "G-d has made laughter for me" (ibid. 21:6). By returning to Hashem in perfect love, she was able to transform and elevate her laughter to become a source of blessing for all (*Sefat Emet*, *Parashat Vayera*, 5652).

Parashat Chayei Sarah

This week's *parashah* (weekly Torah portion) is significant for women, as it portrays the transmission of "the blessings of the tent" from Sarah to Rivkah, the first two of our righteous mothers, the pillars of the house of Israel. Our Torah reading depicts how Sarah handed down the virtues of Jewish womanhood to Rivkah. This began the chain that has been transmitted from generation to generation until today. The more we understand their personalities, the closer our connection to the traditions they established.

Tzaddikim Are Called Alive at Their Death

"Sarah was one hundred and twenty seven years old, these were the years of Sarah's life" (*Bereishit* 23:1). Malbim explains that only when a person passes away can the quality of his life be determined. As long as he is still alive, we never know whether he may come to sin and fall from his previous spiritual level. At Sarah's death, it became known that all of her one hundred and twenty-seven years were equally good, as Rashi learns from the apparently redundant phrase, "*Shenei chayei* Sarah" – "years of Sarah's life." *Bereishit Rabbah* 58:1 praises Sarah's equanimity, "Hashem knows the days of the perfect, and their inheritance is forever." (*Tehillim* 37:18). Just like they are perfect so are their days. Therefore, Avraham lamented over Sarah by reciting the words of the "Woman of Valor" in her praise (*Midrash Tanchuma, Chayei Sarah* 4). Her *temimut* (wholeheartedness/perfection) made Sarah worthy of being eulogized by these verses (*Mishlei* 31:10-31). Written acrostically from the first letter of the Hebrew alphabet *alef* to the final letter *tav,* the verses of the "Woman of Valor" symbolize perfection.

Beyond the Changes of the Time

Sefat Emet explains the words of our *Midrash Rabbah* as follows: It is a great virtue to maintain all our days in equanimity like Sarah. The beginning of her life bore many difficulties such as famine, infertility and being taken captive by Pharaoh and Avimelech. Only at the end of her life did she experience many blessings. Nevertheless, she didn't change with the ups and downs of her life. Therefore, it states about Sarah, "She bestows good and never bad all the days of her life" (*Mishlei* 31:12). Since her perfection was not affected by the changes of time, she was able to withstand any test. By accepting and transforming the negative aspects of her life, she was able to rectify the sin of Chava, who introduced evil into the world.

The Best of All Ages

"One hundred years, twenty years and seven years." Why does the Torah break up the account of Sarah's years as if to say that each period of her life involved a separate entity? According to Rashi, this is in order to teach us that each stage of her life stands on its own. When Sarah was a hundred years old, she was free of sin like a twenty-year-old. At the age of twenty, she was beautiful like a seven-year-old. The age of twenty is usually the prime of beauty, and therefore, Adam and Chava were created at this age (*Bereishit Rabbah* 14:7). Nevertheless, Rabbeinu Bachaya explains that Sarah's beauty continued to increase at the age of twenty, just like a seven-year-old, who is constantly growing and becoming more beautiful. Maharal emphasizes that the Torah does not allude to her physical beauty alone. Sarah's extraordinary beauty teaches us about her spiritual purity. In the same way that Moshe Rabbeinu's spiritual attainments imparted youthful vitality to his body, "Moshe was a hundred and twenty years old when he died; his eye was not dim, nor his natural moisture abated" (*Devarim* 34:7). Likewise, Sarah's spiritual purity enabled her to continually possess the best qualities of all ages.

The Blessings of the Tent

After the death of Sarah, her lack was sorely felt until Rivkah came and revived her spiritual heritage: "Yitzchak brought her into the tent of Sarah his mother, and took Rivkah, and she became his wife. He loved her, and Yitzchak was comforted after his mother's death" (*Bereishit* 24:67). Rashi comments that when he brought her into the tent, she became exactly like his mother Sarah. While Sarah was living, a light burned in the tent from one Shabbat eve to the next. There was a continuous blessing in her dough (symbolizing the blessing of sustenance) and the Cloud of Glory was always hanging over the tent (a sign of Divine protection). Since her death, all of these blessings had ceased. Now that Rivkah entered the tent, they reappeared. According to Maharal, the special *mitzvot* which women perform merit these blessings. The blessing in the dough corresponds to the mitzvah of taking *challah*. The Cloud of Glory derives from the mitzvah of family purity and the burning light from the mitzvah of lighting Shabbat candles.

Extending the Light of Sarah

"The sun rises and the sun sets" (*Kohelet* 1:5). Before Hashem causes the sun of a *tzaddik* (righteous person) to set, he causes the sun of the next *tzaddik* to rise. For this reason, *Parashat Chayei Sarah* is placed next to the announcement of Rivkah's birth. Since the sun of Rivkah had risen, it was time for the sun of Sarah to set (*Bereishit Rabbah* 58:2). *Kli Yakar* reveals that this is also why Yitzchak was praying *minchah* (the afternoon prayer) prior to sunset, when he first met Rivkah. The moment Yitzchak looked up from completing his prayer for a soul mate; Rivkah appeared before his very eyes. This sets an example of the specific power of the *minchah* prayer for a soul mate. Rivkah echoed the quality of Sarah's equanimity and passed it down to all future mothers of Israel, ensuring that there always will be a burning candle in the tent. It is our task as women to shine forth and extend the light of Sarah.

Parashat Toldot

"Yitzchak was forty years old when he took Rivkah, the daughter of Betuel the Aramian of Padanaram, the sister to Lavan the Aramian to be his wife" (*Bereishit* 25:20). Why does the Torah mention the birthplace and genealogy of Rivkah?

A Rose Among Thorns

The Torah mentions Rivkah's family background in order to emphasize how she flourished to become "a rose among thorns" (*Bereishit Rabbah* 63:4). To resist the influence of her environment, Rivkah learned to make her own decisions and to act with complete self-confidence. She was compelled to be assertive, since she grew up in an environment of sinners where it was impossible to rely on anyone, even her own family. Rivkah became familiar with evil without being affected by it. On the contrary, evil drew her towards good, by way of contrast. Her life exemplifies the victory that a person can have over her environment, embodying "...the benefit of the light that emanates [specifically] from the darkness" (*Kohelet* 2:13). Whenever there was a question of what to do, Rivkah took charge. She didn't send her husband to seek Hashem but went by herself. She was the one to receive the Divine message about the reason for her difficult pregnancy and the nature of the children she would birth.

The Pain of Her Pregnancy

"The children struggled together within her; and she said, If it be so, why am I thus? And she went to inquire of Hashem" (*Bereishit* 25:22). After having prayed year after year for a child, Rivkah finally became pregnant – and with twins! However, their struggle against one another, which she felt within her, was almost too much to bear. Rather than rejoicing, she was so disturbed by her discomfort that "she went to inquire of G-d." According to Rashi, Rivkah asked, if the pain of pregnancy is so great, why did I pray and long to become pregnant? *Ohr HaChayim* questions, how this righteous woman could have been disturbed by the discomfort of pregnancy? We know that *tzaddikim* are able to endure great pain in this world, for the sake of eternal goodness. Moreover, when Hashem answered her, "...two nations are in your womb" (ibid. 23), how did that take away the pain of her pregnancy?

To Carry on the Legacy of Sarah

According to Rashi, the answer revealed to Rivkah by Shem (the son of Noach), through *Ruach HaKodesh* (Divine inspiration), is that there were two men of nobility (*gayim*) within her: Antoninus and Rabbi Yehudah the Prince. At first glance, this remark seems totally unrelated the main problem, as the verse continues, "...and two peoples shall be separated from your bowels, the one shall be stronger than the other, and the elder shall serve the younger" (ibid.). Rivkah's consternation must not be merely due to the pain of pregnancy but to something much more devastating. We know that when Yitzchak brought Rivkah into the tent of his mother, Sarah, she completely took over her role. Since they both personified righteousness and holiness, their home became the dwelling place of the *Shechinah* and they were chosen as worthy vessels to generate the future nation of Israel. Then why was Rivkah so upset? According to *Meshech Chochmah*, she was profoundly jealous of Sarah, who had succeeded to select for herself the part of Avraham's seed that was pure and holy to produce Yitzchak. This was after the tinge of Avraham's impurity inherited from his idol-worshipping father had been skimmed away by Hagar to bear Yishmael (*Shabbat* 146a).

Esav – The Hidden Spark Conceived

Rivkah was convinced that she was the bearer of pollution and unholiness. Every time she passed by a place of *avodah zarah* (idol worship), she could feel Esav surging towards that which was utterly despicable to her. It was no consolation that she was also pregnant with "good" as evidenced by the movements in her womb that she noticed upon passing holy places (Rashi, *Bereishit* 25:22). She had somehow failed to live up to the standards set by Sarah and therefore felt devastated. The prophetic answer revealed to her, that within her were the ancestors of two noblemen of a future generation. The first one was Antoninus, the Caesar of Rome a descendant of Esav who converted to Judaism. His good relations with the second one, Rabbi Yehudah, the Prince, enabled the recording of the Oral Law. Thus, Rivkah was assured that even the "bad" contained a tremendous spark of good, which made it worthwhile to be the mother of Esav (*Meshech Chochmah*, *Bereishit* 25:23).

Parashat Vayeitze

In this week's *parashah* two of our greatest mothers are introduced and contrasted: "The eyes of Leah were tender; but Rachel was of beautiful form and of beautiful appearance" (*Bereishit* 29:17). According to Ariza"l, Rachel represents the revealed, whereas Leah corresponds to the hidden world (*Etz Chayim,* Gate 38, Chapter 2).

Leah's Hidden Beauty

Rachel, who was beautiful on all levels, represents the world of the *tzaddik*. Her righteousness illuminated her to such an extent that everyone agreed that she was a striking beauty. One has to look deeper, however, to get in touch with Leah's beauty. The description of Leah's eyes as being soft has puzzled many commentators. Since the eyes are the inner light of the soul, chassidic commentaries explain that Leah represents the world of *teshuvah* (repentance), where beauty is hidden, (see *Ateret Yehoshua* on *Parashat Vayeitze*). Her eyes were soft from crying out to G-d in heartfelt prayer. This prayer enabled her to transcend her destiny and merit to become a partner with her sister in building the house of Israel.

Rachel – The Mother of the Mothers

The first meeting between Ya'acov and Rachel was a romantic encounter of two soul mates who knew they were made for each other. However, in the morning that followed the wedding night, Ya'acov realized that he had married the wrong woman: "It came to pass, that in the morning, behold, it was Leah" (*Bereishit* 29:25). Rashi asks, "Was it not Leah in the evening?" Ya'acov had failed to recognize her until the morning because he had given Rachel certain secret signs that she had transmitted to Leah. When Rachel saw that they were about to substitute Leah in the marriage ceremony, she thought: "My sister may now be put to shame." Therefore, she handed her the secret signs. Rachel's righteousness went beyond anything expected. She was willing not only to share her beloved but also to give up the entire dream of her future life with Ya'acov. How was she to know that she would merit to become Ya'acov's wife as well? In her selfless concern that her sister not be embarrassed, she sacrificed her own future and enabled Leah to become a mother in Israel. In this way, Rachel became the embodiment of motherhood – the mother of all mothers.

Mutual Love

"When Rachel saw that she bore Ya'acov no children, Rachel became jealous of her sister" (*Bereishit* 30:1). Knowing Rachel's concern and love for her sister, how could she possibly sink down to the low level of envy? Rashi explains that she was jealous of Leah's good deeds, the only kind of jealousy permitted. Instead of begrudging someone else what they have and feeling that they don't deserve it, Rachel believed that her sister merited children because she was on a higher spiritual level. The love between the sisters was reciprocal. Leah showed her gratitude to Rachel by praying for her to conceive. When Leah became pregnant for the seventh time, she was concerned that if it was a boy, only one of the twelve tribes would be left for Rachel. Through her heart-piercing prayer she was able to change the sex of her fetus, and enable Rachel to give birth to two of the important tribes of Israel, Yosef and Binyamin (Rashi, *Bereishit* 30:21).

Together We Can Build the House of Israel

The unity between Rachel and Leah reverberates throughout the ages. Today, more than ever, we need to link ourselves with their love for one another in order to overcome division and jealousy among the Jewish people. In the messianic era, we will have the task of bringing down the "hidden lights" of Leah into the "rectified vessels" of Rachel.

Leah was originally destined for Esav. In spite of his wickedness, many righteous converts descended from him. The souls of Rabbi Akiva, son of the converts, Shemayah and Avtaliyon, and the grandchildren of Haman in B'nei Berak were trapped within Esav (see *Gittin* 57b, *Sanhedrin* 96b). Through her marriage to Ya'acov, Leah became like a bridge between Esav and Ya'acov. She rectified the holy souls among Esav's descendants, allowing their hidden lights to shine forth by enabling their passage from the side of Esav to the fold of Ya'acov – through their conversion. It was the power of Leah's *teshuvah* that extracted these holy sparks from within the darkness. By rectifying herself and the part of Esav that she embodied, Leah was able to free them from his trap. The righteousness of Rachel was not sufficient to absorb these souls. Leah set the precedent for all righteous converts to issue from Esav. Without her, these souls would have remained trapped in the other side represented by Esav.

We need to walk in the footsteps of our mothers and include aspects of both Rachel and Leah within ourselves. Our primary endeavor should be to become righteous like Rachel. However, we need to include Leah's hidden world of *teshuvah* as well. This entails tolerance of others who may be completely different from us. Even if they may seem far from perfect on the surface, we need to look for their hidden sparks. By bridging the different segments within the people of Israel, we share in the building of our everlasting Temple, initiated by the unconditional love of our mothers. This is one reason why the Temple – may it be rebuilt in our days! – is located on the border between the Land of Binyamin, son of Rachel, and the Land of Yehudah, son of Leah. Only through the united power of Rachel and Leah is it possible to elevate all the souls of Israel. "Like Rachel and like Leah, who both built the house of Israel" (*Ruth* 4:11).

Parashat Vayislach

The story of Dinah teaches us how careful a Jewish woman must be to protect herself against harassment. Rabbi Ezriel Tauber compares the woman to a diamond and the man to a ring. A ring without a diamond has very little value, yet a diamond without a ring although it has great value, can easily get lost. Therefore, it must be kept in a secure place.

Like Mother Like Daughter

"Dinah the daughter of Leah, whom she bore to Ya'acov went out to see the daughters of the land" (*Bereishit* 34:1). Abarbanel asks why we need this detailed description of Dinah. Was there another Dinah that it was necessary to state "daughter of Leah whom she bore unto Ya'acov"? Rashi answers that the saying "like mother like daughter" originally applied to Dinah. She is called the daughter of Leah since she, too, was outgoing, as it states: "Leah went out towards him" (*Bereishit* 30:16).

This comparison does not come to denigrate Dinah, as Abarbanel explains. At first, when Ya'acov intended to marry Rachel, but instead was given Leah, he did not recognize her until the next morning, because of Leah's modesty (*Bereishit* 29:25). When she later went out towards Ya'acov and said, "...you must come to me" (*Bereishit* 30:16), her intention was for the sake of Heaven to bear his children and raise the tribes of Israel. The proof is that she merited, that same night, to conceive Yissaschar, who represents Torah (Rashi, *Bereishit* 49:14, 15).

Dinah, likewise, did not have improper intentions. She only wanted to watch the daughters of the land and not the men of the city. She longed to see the clothes and the jewelry of other girls and learn the way of young women, since there were no other girls in Ya'acov's house. *Ohr HaChayim* explains that "Dinah went out to see the daughters of the land," because Shechem had brought girls around Ya'acov's tent who would play harp and make fanfare in order to entice Dinah.

Ya'acov's Only Daughter

Rabbeinu Bachaya explains that the reason why the Torah states, "whom she bore unto Ya'acov" is to allude to the fact that Ya'acov was partly to blame for what happened to his daughter. He withheld Dinah from Esav, although she possibly could have made him repent. The Midrash teaches that Ya'acov placed Dinah in a box when Esav came towards him, so that Esav would not put his eyes on her. Hashem said, "You did not want her to marry someone circumcised; she will be taken by someone uncircumcised. You did not want her to be married in a permissive way; she will be taken in a forbidden way" (*Bereishit Rabbah* 76:9).

In Dinah's Praise

"When Shechem, the son of Chamor, the Chivite, prince of the country, saw her, he took her, lay with her, and afflicted her" (*Bereishit* 24:2). According to Rabbi S.R. Hirsch, although Dinah became desecrated, she remained entirely the daughter of Ya'acov. Malbim notes how it states that Shechem saw her, to teach us that it was not Dinah who initiated the conversation. As soon as Shechem saw her, he took her by force. Ramban credits Dinah for not being interested in the prince of the land and describes how she screamed and cried constantly. Otherwise Shechem would not have needed to ask his father "...take for me this girl for a wife" (*Bereishit* 34:4) since the girl was already in his possession and as the prince of the land he had no need to fear that anyone would take her away from him. Yet, because of Dinah's resistance towards him, he tried to bribe her family to convince her to concede willingly to the match (Ramban, *Bereishit* 34:12).

The Insides of the Daughters of the Land

In Hebrew, the word *et* is used to indicate that the word following a verb becomes the object of the sentence. Therefore, we would have expected the word *et* in "Dinah went out to see [*et*] the daughters of the land." *Be'er Mayim Chayim* notes that the letter *beit*, which means "in" is used instead of the *et*. This makes the verse read, "Dinah went out to see **inside** the daughters of the land." Dinah went out to see the inner depths of the hearts of the gentile girls in order to learn who would be receptive to her influence. She understood that also among the gentiles, there are souls capable of becoming purified and clinging to Israel, as is known from Ruth and other converts. Thus the Torah praises Dinah. She went explicitly to see and not to be seen. She did not care to show off her beauty. However, when Sarah converted women, she did so from within her tent. She waited for the women to come to her. On the other hand, Yael the Kenite also went out and Devorah praised her and called her, "More blessed than women of the tent" (*Shoftim* 5:24). This teaches us that there is a way for a modest woman to "go out" and benefit the world without being harmed.

Her Jewish Essence Remains Pure

What happened to the child that Dinah conceived from her encounter with Shechem ben Chamor? Yonatan ben Uziel in his translation of *Bereishit* 41:45 identifies Osenat as "Dinah's daughter whom she bore to Shechem." In spite of the tainted nature of her conception, Osenat became the wife of Yosef the *tzaddik*. As Yosef's soul mate, she was like him, sealed with complete sexual chastity. She, moreover, merited to become the mother of Efrayim and Menasheh, two tribes considered equal in holiness to the sons of Ya'acov. This testifies that the inner essence of Osenat's mother, Dinah, remained unaffected and pure even when she was defiled by Shechem (Rabbi Tzadok of Lublin, *Yisrael Kedoshim* 10). The power of her innate holiness is, furthermore, expressed on a global level as she affects the circumcision of the entire city.

The DNA of Hashem

Dinah's daughter, Osenat, is the first person through whom it becomes established that the Jewish lineage follows the mother. In this way, Dinah teaches us that no matter which kinds of experiences a Jewish woman may have gone through in her past; there is a place within her soul that remains completely intact and pure in its holiness. This holy spark is carried on to the children she conceives. My friend Esther Linder told me a hint for the fact that we learn from Dinah that Judaism follows the mother: Dinah's name consists of the letters D, N, and A plus the letter H or Hebrew letter *heh* that represents Hashem. Thus Dinah represents "the DNA of Hashem."

Parashat Vayeishev

We have just learned from the incident of Dinah how careful a woman needs to be to protect herself. Nevertheless, Tamar goes out to sit by the crossroads, where everyone passes, in order to seduce Yehudah. Not only is she unharmed, but she is even rewarded by conceiving the sprout of Mashiach.

Outer Disgrace – Inner Praise

"It was told to Tamar, saying, behold your father-in-law goes up to Timnah to shear his sheep. She put off her widow's garments, and covered herself with a veil, wrapped herself, and sat by the entrance to Einayim, which is by the way to Timnah; for she saw that Sheilah was grown, and she was not given to him as a wife" (*Bereishit* 38:13–14). According to Abarbanel, the many coincidences that led to the union between Yehudah and Tamar alluded to the fact that Hashem was at work behind the scenes. Malbim explains that besides discerning that Sheilah had grown, Tamar also realized that Yehudah's wife had died and that he was, therefore, free to fulfill the mitzvah of *yibum* (levirate marriage). It was, moreover, clear to her that Yehudah had already been consoled, since he went up to shear his sheep, an event usually accompanied by joyous partying. Tamar sat at Petach Einayim (the Entrance of the Eye) in order to meet Yehudah and convince him to marry her. *Sforno* points out that her intentions were for the sake of Heaven. She prophetically understood that Mashiach had to be born from the union between herself and Yehudah, for he was more perfect than Sheilah.

The Angel of Her Prayer

"He turned to her by the way, and said, Come now, please, let me come in to you, (for he knew not that she was his daughter-in-law)" (ibid. 16). The Torah did not state the usual "He went to her," but rather "He turned to her." *Da'at Zekeinim* explains that Yehudah wanted to pass her by, when Tamar lifted her eyes and prayed, "*Ribon HaOlamim*, (Master of the Universe) do I not have the merit to bring forth a wise son from this *tzaddik*?" Immediately G-d sent the angel Michael to turn him back. Thus, Tamar's prayers had the power to create an angel that influenced the will of Yehudah. As the Midrash says, "Yehudah wanted to pass on, when Hashem sent the angel in charge of physical desire. He said to him; Yehudah where are you going? Where are kings standing? And from where do the great come forth? 'He turned to her by the way' (*Bereishit* 38:16) – against his will" (*Bereishit Rabbah* 85:8).

The Heart of a Lioness

"It came to pass about three months after, that it was told to Yehudah, saying, Tamar your daughter-in-law has played the harlot; and also, behold, she is with child by harlotry. And Yehudah said, bring her out, and let her be burned" (*Bereishit* 38:24). Although they were taking her to be burned, Tamar didn't try to defend herself, because she had the heart of a lioness. She preferred endangering her life rather than embarrassing Yehudah. She could have removed any suspicion from herself by directly stating that she was pregnant from Yehudah. (*Sforno*, *Bereishit* 38:25). From Tamar, our sages learn that a person should rather let himself be burned than embarrass someone in public (Rashi, ad loco). She could, however, have saved herself from danger while simultaneously avoiding embarrassing Yehudah in public by simply explaining the whole matter to Yehudah privately.

Becoming Worthy of Mashiach

According to Rabbi Eliyahu Kitov, Tamar understood that certain matters still had to be purified before her sons could see the light of the world. Both she and Yehudah needed to prove that they deserved to become parents of kings. She had to be willing to sacrifice her life, rather than cause embarrassment to a fellow Jew, and Yehudah had to renounce his honor, for the sake of truth. Tamar realized that if these two *tikunim* (rectifications) were not made she would have no further purpose in the world and death would be unavoidable. If, however, she could demonstrate strength and willingness to lose everything, and Yehudah would be willing to undergo immense embarrassment by publicly admitting that he was wrong, his humiliation would then be transformed to everlasting honor. For this reason, Tamar took upon herself the difficult test of keeping the whole truth to herself. She understood that the difference between complete destruction and total bliss depends on a hair's breadth. When Tamar learned that Yehudah went up to Timnah, the Torah states, "It was told to Tamar." The same language, "It was told to Yehudah" informed him that Tamar was pregnant. This alludes to the fact that the same *maggid* (heavenly reporter) was sent to test them both. Each of them was given the opportunity to prove that they were worthy to become parents of Mashiach.

More Righteous "from Me"

Yehudah passed his test when he publicly announced Tamar's righteousness. His exclamation: "*Tzadkah mimeni!*" is usually translated, "She is more righteous than me" (*Bereishit* 38:26). Yet, it can also be understood, "She is righteous. From me – (*mimeni*) [is she pregnant]." A third possibility is that the word "from me" is proclaimed by a Heavenly voice: "From Me and by My agency have these things happened." Since she proved herself a modest woman while in her father-in-law's house, I have ordained that kings shall descend from her. I have already ordained that kings shall rise up in Israel from the tribe of Yehudah. Therefore, I have brought it about that these two persons who are to be the ancestors of kings should unite (Rashi ad loco, based on *Bereishit Rabbah* 85:12).

Humble Origins

Rabbi Eliyahu Kitov explains that when Hashem was planting the first sprout of the Kingdom of Israel, He ensured it would be planted with no one's intentions but His own. The king brought into being in this manner would remain unassuming because of his humble origin. Sometimes deeds that seem immoral are completely pure and for the sake of Heaven. Actually, most of the circumstances instrumental in bringing Mashiach seem on the surface, to be anything but holy; from the incident of Lot's daughters and Tamar dressed up as a harlot to Ruth the Moabitess lying down on the threshing floor at Boaz's feet. The holier something is the more obstacles prevent it from being carried out. The only way to circumvent the negative forces is through disguise, like Tamar, as the *Chafetz Chayim* teaches:

> *The lesson of the story is that the Satan prevents the most high and lofty matters. Therefore, there is no other advice except to make the way crooked. In the straight way, the Satan would have accused and nothing could have been achieved. The same is true of Oved, the grandfather of David, who came forth from Ruth the Moabitess* (*Chafetz Chayim* on the Torah, *Parashat Vayeishev*).

While it is not our job to deliberately "make the way crooked," we must learn not to judge others as G-d brings about the sprout of Mashiach in unexpected and hidden ways.

Parashat Mikeitz

"Pharaoh called Yosef's name Zaphnath-pa'neach; and he gave him Osenat the daughter of Poti-fera priest of On as a wife" (*Bereishit* 41:45).

Who Was Osenat?

As we explained in *Parashat Vayishlach* (on page 29), Osenat was Dinah's daughter, born from her incident with Shechem. Why did Shechem desire Dinah so much? Rabbi Tzadok HaKohen explains in *Yisrael Kedoshim* that although the cursed Shechem and the blessed Dinah had nothing in common to bind them together, Shechem desired her because there was a certain spark of holiness within him that Dinah was able to redeem. From their union came forth the holy soul of Osenat, destined to be the soul mate of the righteous Yosef.

According to *Chizkuni*, Ya'acov sent Osenat away to protect her from Dinah's brothers. Since she was the product of sin, they were not aware of her redeeming qualities. Ya'acov, however, realized that Jewish lineage follows the mother. Rabbeinu Bachaya explains that she was called Osenat from the Hebrew word *seneh*, which means bush (referring to her hiding place). It is also possible that her name is related to the Hebrew word *senuah* which means hated.

The Seed of Ya'acov

Before sending Osenat away, Ya'acov tied an amulet on her neck, upon which was written, "whoever cleaves to you, cleaves to the seed of Ya'acov" (*Targum Onkelos, Parashat Vayechi* 48:9). *Chizkuni* adds that the angel Gavriel brought her to Egypt to the house of Potifar, who adopted her. When Yosef ruled over Egypt, all the women wanted to gaze at him because of his good looks, as it states: "…daughters tread on the wall" (*Bereishit* 49:22). Each of them would cast something down from the wall as a gift for Yosef. Since Osenat had nothing else to throw, she hurled the amulet from around her neck. In this way, when Yosef saw that she was the granddaughter of Ya'acov, he married her.

Yosef's Perfect Match

Yosef's marriage to Osenat made it known that he had not sinned with her mother. The fact that Potifar agreed to give his daughter's hand to Yosef in marriage shows that he conceded to Yosef's innocence. For who would be willing to marry off his daughter to the man who had violated her mother? Osenat saved Yosef's life (*Yalkut Shimoni, Bereishit* 39:146). She testified to her father that Yosef did not seduce her mother. *Da'at Zekeinim* notes that it was by a complete miracle that Osenat wound up in Egypt, in order that Yosef would discover her. Osenat grew up in an environment that was all but conducive to holiness. She was adopted and raised by Potifar's wife in a society known for its sexual perversity. Although she was the product of violation by the uncircumcised Shechem, nevertheless, she maintained her purity and holiness and so became the perfect match for Yosef, who is known for his ability to overcome sexual temptation (*Bereishit* 39:13).

Guarding the Covenant of Circumcision

Besides being able to control his own sexuality, Yosef, moreover, attempted to dissolve the shell of the foreskin from the entire world, by ordering the Egyptians who wished to buy food to circumcise themselves in exchange (see Rashi, *Bereishit* 41:55). Being Yosef's soul mate and partner in his mission, Osenat's righteousness was also connected to the holiness of the circumcision. Although the covenant of circumcision does not pertain physically to a Jewish daughter, it affects her on a much deeper spiritual level, imbuing her inner essence with an inherent purity that can never be tainted. While a Jewish male must undergo circumcision to receive an increased connection to G-d, this connection is inherent in women. Therefore, the Jewish daughter is internally connected to the covenant of circumcision to the extent that an uncircumcised gentile will not be able to defile neither her, nor the child conceived. This explains why Judaism is transmitted through the mother.

According to the *Zohar*, after Adam was expelled from Eden, he pulled his foreskin forward to hide the sign of the covenant. A rectification for this sin was enacted through the deed that brought the soul of Osenat into the world, requiring that every male be circumcised (*Bereishit* 34:24). Osenat is another example of pure and holy *neshamot* (souls) brought into being through unholy circumstances in order to fool the Satan (see *Chafetz Chayim* on *Parashat Vayeishev*). Their ability to withstand even the darkest obstacles brings forth and actualizes their true holiness to become the greatest light.

Parashat Vayigash

Serach is the only granddaughter, and the only woman besides Ya'acov's immediate family included in the enumeration of the seventy souls of Ya'acov's house who descended down to Egypt: "The children of Asher...and Serach their sister" (*Bereishit* 46:17). Her name appears again two hundred and fifty years later among the names of the family of Asher who were to receive a portion in the Land of Israel.

Serach Bat Asher – Her Days Were Twined and Multiplied

"The daughter of Asher was Serach" (*Bemidbar* 26:46). Rashi remarks, "Because she was still alive, she is counted here." Asher was blessed that his old age would be like the days of his youth (*Devarim* 33:24). The length of the life of Serach, his daughter, however, by far exceeded the life span of anyone else in her tribe, including her father. The meaning of her name is appropriate to her extraordinary longevity. The name "Serach" means to twist, traverse, twine, lace, stretch, spread out, hang over and be dragged. Thus, our sages relate that she was called Serach because "*sheserachu v'nitrabu yemeiha*" – her days were twined and multiplied.

Bridging the Transitions of Israel

Serach played a key role in bringing the children of Israel down to Egypt. Yosef's brothers were concerned about how best to reveal to their aging father that his favorite son was still alive, without shocking him by the astounding news. According to our tradition, Serach bat Asher solved their problem. By gently playing the harp and singing, "Yosef is still alive, Yosef is still alive," she revived the spirit of Ya'acov, her grandfather. In this way, Serach was instrumental in reuniting Ya'acov with Yosef and bringing his entire family to Egypt. She also had a central part in delivering the Jewish people out of the Egyptian exile. Serach was the one to assure the children of Israel that Moshe was their true redeemer. They had a tradition from Ya'acov that any redeemer who would come and say, *Pacod Pacadeti Etchem*, (I have surely visited you) is a true redeemer. Ya'acov handed this secret over to Yosef, Yosef to his brothers, and Asher the son of Ya'acov handed the secret over to his daughter, Serach, who was still alive during Moshe's time. Therefore, the Jewish people immediately believed Moshe when he pronounced this phrase (*Shemot Rabbah* 5:13). The Maharzav comments that just like Serach was still alive at the time of the redemption from Egypt, so will she continue to exist in the future.

The Peaceful and Faithful of Israel

Serach's life continued during King David's kingdom. She was the wise woman who prevented a civil war in Israel, as it states: "Then cried a wise woman out of the city…When he approached her, the woman said, Are you Yoav?" (2 *Shemuel* 20:16–17). According to *Bereishit Rabbah* 94:9, she said, "By causing bloodshed among Israel, you do not live up to your name Yoav, which means a father to Israel." When Yoav questioned, "Who are you?" she replied, "I am the peaceful and faithful of Israel" (ibid. 19). "I am the one who completed the numbers of Israel in Egypt. I am the one who connected the faithful Yosef to Moshe. How can you desire to kill a city and me who is a mother in Israel?" Immediately Yoav answered and said, "Far be it, far be it from me" (ibid. 20). In this way, Serach upheld the Kingdom of David against the rebellion of Sheva ben Bichri, the last movement of resistance to David's kingdom.

Reaching Beyond Divisions

Serach's continued involvement with the unity of Israel extends even to the time of the Talmud: "Rabbi Yochanan was sitting and learning how the water became like a wall for Israel at the splitting of the sea. He understood it to be like wooden latticework. Then Serach peeked out from the Garden of Eden and said, "I was there, and the waters were nothing but clear, lit up windows" (*Yalkut Shimoni*, 2 *Shemuel* 20:152). Serach did not tolerate any separation between the tribes. When the people of Israel crossed the Sea of Reeds, there was neither fence nor wooden lattice. Without divisions, the different tribes saw each other clearly while passing through. Just as they went down to Egypt as one people, so did they arise from Egypt as one people, seeing each other through the up lit windows. By reaching beyond the divisions of Israel, Serach was able to guide the Jewish people during the crucial turning points of our history. She completed the numbers of the people who went to Egypt, announced the right time for leaving Egypt, and crushed the last resistance against King David. The continuing existence of Serach affirms that the quest for unity and peace is always alive within Jewish womanhood. Serach transmits the melody of life and redemption through the righteous women of each generation. Let us join her quiet yet powerful tune!

Parashat Vayechi

At his deathbed, it was difficult for Ya'acov to request from Yosef to bring his remains into the Land of Israel. Ramban explains that Ya'acov needed to justify his request to be buried in the Cave of Machpelah to Yosef, since he didn't bury Rachel, Yosef's mother, there: "As for me, when I came from Paddan, Rachel died by me in the Land of Canaan on the way, when there was but a *kibrat* of land to come into Efrat; and I buried her there on the way of Efrat, which is Beitlechem" (*Bereishit* 48:7).

Buried by the Wayside

Why did Ya'acov let his favorite wife lie by the wayside, instead of carrying her at least into the city of Beitlechem, which was nearby? According to Ramban, the reason why Ya'acov didn't bury Rachel in the Cave of Machpelah was in order that he should not be buried together with two sisters, for Torah law forbids marrying two sisters. Since Leah was his first wife, she was buried with Ya'acov, despite the fact that Rachel was his first love. Rashi explains the deeper reason why Rachel had to be buried by the wayside. Ya'acov buried her there by the command of G-d, so that Rachel would help her children in future times when Nebuzaradan would drive them into captivity. When the Jews were to pass along the road, Rachel would come forth from her grave and stand by her tomb weeping and beseeching mercy for her children:

> *Thus says Hashem, A voice was heard in Ramah, lamentation and bitter weeping, Rachel weeping for her children, she refused to be comforted for her children, because they are not. Thus says Hashem, Keep your voice from weeping and your eyes from tears; for your deed shall be rewarded says Hashem; and they shall come back again from the land of the enemy. There is hope for your future, says Hashem, that your children shall come back again to their own border* (*Yirmeyahu* 31:14–16).

For the Sake of Rachel

Why is Rachel specifically called the mother of Israel? Rabbi Shimon ben Yochai said that since everything is dependent on Rachel, the children of Israel are considered hers, as it states: "Rachel is weeping for her children" (*Bereishit Rabbah* 71:2 quoting *Yirmeyahu* 31:14). Rachel is foremost in building the house of Israel. In her selflessness, she enabled Leah to become a mother as well. The entire Jewish people came into being through Rachel's doing. Therefore, G-d assures their return and continued existence for the sake of Rachel.

> *When our ancestors went to appease G-d for Menasheh's sin of having brought an idol into the sanctuary of the Temple, none of their pleads had any effect until Rachel entered and said before G-d, "Master of the Universe whose mercy is greater, Yours or the mercy of people of flesh and blood? Isn't your mercy greater? However, didn't I bring a rival into my house? All the years that Ya'acov worked for my father, he only worked for me. When I came to enter the chuppah, (marriage canopy) they brought my sister in my place. Not only did I keep silent, I even handed her over my secret signs. Likewise You, if your children brought Your rival into your house, keep silent to them." G-d answered her, "You have defended your children beautifully. There is reward for your deed and righteousness that you handed over your secret signs to your sister"* (Rashi, *Yirmeyahu* 31:14).

The Power of Prayer Depends on Deeds

It is difficult for us to appreciate the greatness of Rachel's deed. Perhaps we might consider her to be so righteous that she is completely above the natural trait of jealousy, which would prevent most of us from being willing to share our husbands with anyone, even with our sister. However, the Torah comes to witness that this is not the case. When Rachel remained childless while her sister Leah bore one son after the other, she was overcome with jealousy: "When Rachel saw that she bore Ya'acov no children, Rachel was jealous of her sister" (*Bereishit* 30:1).

According to *Kli Yakar*, during the long years of Rachel's childlessness, she searched her soul for some kind of sin that might cause G-d to withhold the fruits of her womb. She didn't find any sin except the trace of jealousy. She therefore concluded that it was this sin that prevented her and Ya'acov's *tefilah* (prayer) from being accepted. She then decided to repent and overcome her jealousy to the extent that she would be willing to bring her maidservant into her husband's bosom without becoming jealous. Therefore, she said, "In the merit that I brought my rival (Bilhah) into my house, I will also be built through her" (*Kli Yakar, Bereishit* 30:2).

Rachel teaches us that the power of our prayer is dependent on the merit of our deeds. It is not only our intention at the moment of prayer that enables our supplication to pierce through the heavens and enter the Seat of Glory. Rachel's bitter weeping was heard in the Heaven above because of her former acts of righteousness. Ya'acov was the dream of Rachel's life, and she knew that she was destined for him. Nevertheless, she handed over her secret signs to Leah and thereby willingly renounced the fulfillment of her dream, including the eternal rest with her beloved. Her self-effacement and sacrifice stands as an everlasting merit for the Jewish people throughout the ages.

The Book of Shemot – Names (Exodus)

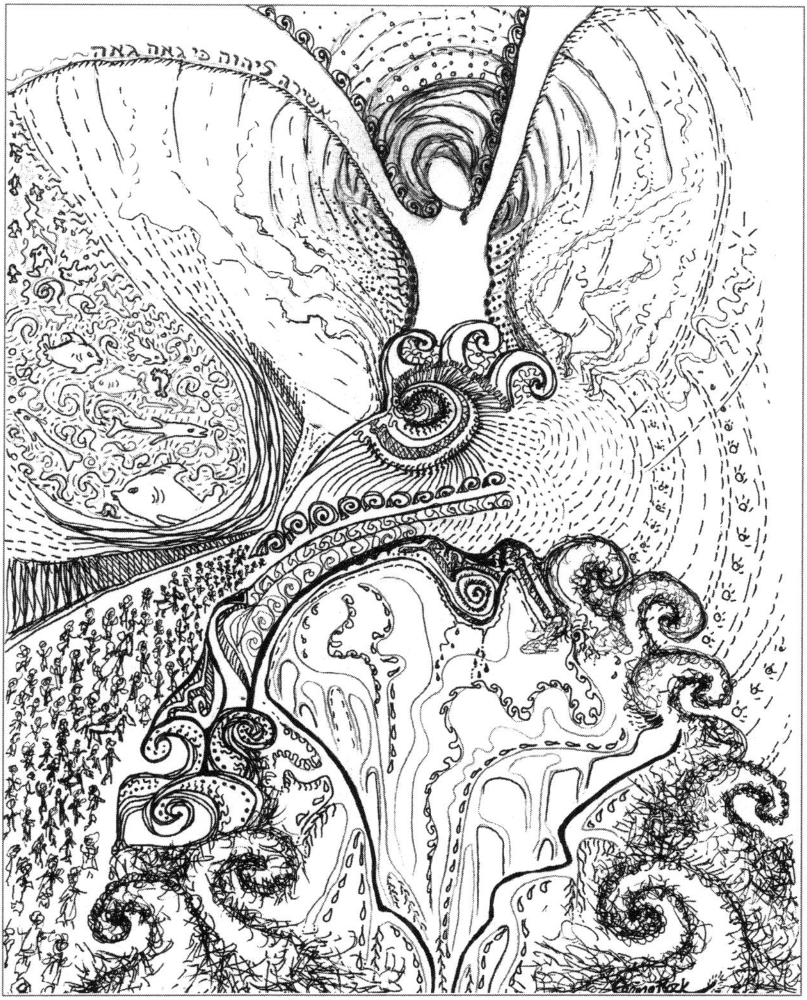

Parashat Shemot

"Israel was redeemed from Egypt in the merit of the righteous women from that generation" (*Sotah* 11b). Learning about the Jewish midwives who played an important role in the redemption from the Egyptian exile can inspire us to help bring about the future redemption.

Who Were the Midwives in Egypt?

"The King of Egypt spoke to the Hebrew midwives, of whom the name of the one was Shifrah, and the name of the second Puah" (*Shemot* 1:15). Considering the immense population explosion among the Jews during the Egyptian exile, the obvious question arises: How is it possible that two midwives could be sufficient for a nation as great as Israel? Ibn Ezra explains that these two were in charge of all the midwives; for without doubt there were more than five hundred midwives. According to Abarbanel, there were two types of midwives. The Shifrah-type would take care of the baby, and clean it, while the Puah-type would help the woman in labor with her breathing and prayer. Rashi's explains, based on *Sotah* 11b that Shifrah, from the language of *meshaperet,* which means to improve, was another name for Yocheved. She used to take care of the baby after its birth and put it into good physical condition. Puah was another name for Miriam. She used to speak aloud and croon to the baby just as women do to soothe a child from crying. *Maharsha* explains that the language "...the name of **the one**...and the name of **the second...**" is never found in the Torah unless it has previously stated that there were two people. As for example, "Unto Ever were born **two sons**, the name of the one was Peleg...and the name of the second..." (*Bereishit* 10:25). Yet, regarding Shifrah and Puah it states, "...the name of **the one** was Shifrah, and the name of **the second** was Puah," using the definite article without prefacing that there were two Hebrew midwives. From this, *Maharsha* deducts that their identities must have been known from another place in the Torah. This is how we know that Shifrah and Puah must be Yocheved and Miriam, the most well known women in their time.

The Names of Their Faith

Kli Yakar reveals that Puah, the language of speaking, refers to Miriam because she spoke in prophecy, as it states: "Miriam the prophetess, the sister of Aharon" (*Shemot* 15:20). She prophesied saying, "In the future my mother will give birth to a son who will redeem Israel." Shifrah is Yocheved who returned to the beauty (*shofrah*) of her youth when she was one hundred and thirty years old. This miracle was a sign that she would give birth to Moshe, the redeemer of Israel, because a miracle is never performed without reason. The Torah, therefore, uses these names to emphasize that the redeemer would come forth through them. Since these names are associated with miracles and redemption, they are also used to show how the midwives did not doubt the redemption. Without their steadfast belief in the forthcoming redemption, they might not have been able to refuse Pharaoh's command, rationalizing that it would be better for the children to die young, than to grow up to a life full of pain and servitude.

Like the Animals of the Field

"The midwives said unto Pharaoh, the Hebrew women are not as the Egyptian women, for they are vigorous (*chayot*) and bear before the midwives come unto them" (*Shemot* 1:19). The word *chayot* needs explanation. Since the word *chayata* in Aramaic means midwife, Rashi explains that the Jewish women were experts in midwifery. In Hebrew the word *chayot* literally means animals. Thus, the Talmud explains that the Jewish women were like animals that do not need anyone to help them give birth (*Sotah* 11b). What are we to learn from this comparison? Certain aspects of the life of animals can teach us how to become closer to G-d. Living from hand-to-mouth, as animals do, can help us experience Hashem's providence in this world. It can make us aware when G-d sends the paycheck exactly when the bill is due. The more we protect ourselves with fancy houses, life insurance, etc., the more of a barrier we build between Hashem and ourselves. Living in simple quarters makes us more dependent on G-d's protection.

A Rectification for Chava's Sin

By acting in accordance with the will of G-d, the Jewish people have the ability to overcome the limitations decreed upon Adam and Chava as a result of their sin. *Be'er Mayim Chayim* explains that the pain of childbirth, (*Bereishit* 3:16), derives from the spiritual impurity (*zehumah*) which the snake injected into Chava. The *zehumah* will not allow her to give birth easily and bring more people into the world, since spiritual impurity thrives in desolate places, devoid of people: "A house in which no one lives – destructive spirits live there" (Rashi, *Baba Kama* 2a). Our sages teach that the righteous women in Egypt overcame the curse of Chava and purified themselves from her *zehumah*. Their holiness enabled them to give birth easily, since holiness desires to increase the seed of Israel. Had Adam named his wife Chava only because she was the mother of all life, he should have called her Chaya. However, the name Chava also derives from the word *chiviah*, which means serpent in Aramaic. When Chava succumbed to the temptation of the serpent, it injected its *zehumah* within her. The righteous women in Egypt, who had purified themselves from the *zehumah* of the snake, were therefore called *Chayot* – restoring what originally would have been the name of the first woman.

Giving Birth to the Nation of Israel

The simple faith and righteousness of the Jewish midwives together with all the Jewish women who continued to bear children, helped them withstand the torturous suffering of slavery, and brought about the redemption. Their desire for life gave birth to the entire Jewish nation, while their hope and trust in the redemption helped make it happen. Similarly, today we can take part in manifesting the Heavenly Kingdom through faith, prayer, and action. One way to demonstrate our steadfast belief is to bear many children, and participate in building the Land of Israel. Even if our aspirations seem to go against the decrees of the leaders of the world, even if the world seems dark and clouded, like Shifrah and Puah, we will continue to strengthen our faith in Hashem and the nation of Israel.

Parashat Vaera

In contrast to the women, the Jewish men were unable to hear about the forthcoming redemption, because of the heavy burden of their servitude. "Moshe spoke to the children of Israel, but they did not listen to Moshe through anguish of spirit and through hard service" (*Shemot* 6:10).

The Bitterness of Their Spirit

People of bitter spirit cannot think about anything except how to satisfy their immediate needs. They are looking for instant relief alone, and do not have the *menuchat hanefesh* (ease of mind) it takes to envision redemption or to yearn for freedom. All they can think of is how to provide for their next meal.

The Exile of Speech

"Behold the children of Israel have not listened to me; how then shall Pharaoh hear me, who am of uncircumcised lips?" (*Shemot* 6:12). *Sefat Emet* explains that there is a direct connection between the prophet's ability to prophesize and the people's capacity to listen. The reason why Moshe was of uncircumcised lips was because Israel could not listen to him. It was this inability of the Jewish people to listen, which prevented them from receiving the Ten Commandments directly from G-d. Speech is in exile as long as the receivers are not prepared to listen to the Divine word. The Midrash explains that Israel could not listen to Moshe, because it was difficult for them to separate themselves from idol worship (*Shemot Rabbah* 6:5). The term for idol worship in Hebrew is *avodah zarah*, which literally means strange work. Therefore, any kind of compulsion for "strange work" other than Hashem's *mitzvot* can block our ability to hear the voice of G-d.

Sometimes, I find it hard to separate myself from cleaning the very last dish, even if it will make me late for an important meeting. We need to pull ourselves away from the obsession with perfectly completing each professional or domestic chore. Situations may arise when our full attention is needed for something more important, whether a baby's insistent cry or an adolescent child who wants to talk about feelings. In each case, we must stop and listen to the voice of Hashem within, and ask ourselves, what does Hashem want from me most right now?

There is a true story about one of the greatest violinists in the world, Joshua Bell playing incognito at Washington, DC Metro Station on a cold January morning in 2007. He played one of the most intricate pieces ever written, with a violin worth 3.5 million dollars. About two thousand people went through the station, yet only six people stopped and listened for a short while. If we do not have a moment to stop and listen to one of the best musicians in the world, playing some of the finest music ever written, with one of the most beautiful instruments ever made how many other Divine wonders of the world are we missing?

Before sinning, Adam and Chava lived in the Garden of Eden where they could enjoy its fruits without having to work. They were free to devote themselves completely to listening to the voice of G-d. Since they misused this opportunity, it was taken away from them. From then on, man was cursed to work to earn a living by the sweat of his brow. In the same way that the men in Egypt were unable to hear the words of redemption, in our times, being excessively caught up in hard work can prevent people from hearing the inner voice of G-d.

The Women Were Able to Hear

The Jewish women in Egypt were able to see beyond their momentary enslavement. Servitude did not drag them down so low that they forgot about the possibility of freedom. In spite of the bitterness of their situation, they were able to envision the future redemption. Therefore, they are praised for enticing their husbands to have relations with them in order to bear children. While the men had given up hope, the women believed in a better future. They saw their situation in perspective and understood that whatever they had to tolerate at the moment, was only a tiny piece in the great puzzle of life.

Hearing the Voice

The main challenge of exile is to free our mind from all external matters, in order to be able to truly listen. *Sefat Emet* urges us to detach ourselves from the emptiness of materialism in order to free our hearts to listen to the words of G-d. Although a woman is busy with all kinds of mundane tasks from office work to sweeping the floor, it is our attitude that makes the difference. It is a unique feminine capability to be able to operate in more than one dimension at a time. Physical work does not take away from our capacity to listen and see our task within the context of a greater perspective. Being overly caught up in physical work by the sweat of our brow is not the women's way. Women do not need to partake of the curse of man.

Transcending Enslavement to Give Ear

During our morning prayer, we mention the Exodus from Egypt before *Shema Yisrael*. By freeing ourselves from the enslavement of Egypt and all other foreign cultures as well, we become ready to hear the word of G-d. The Israelites "did not listen to Moshe through anguish of spirit, and through hard work," because their physical needs dominated their soul. Worrying too much about being physically comfortable can make us ignore the suffering of our soul. G-d gave us the gift of an extra soul on Shabbat in order to free ourselves from the enslavement of our body. Likewise, refraining from the thirty-nine *melachot* (creative works) on Shabbat enables us to hear the word of G-d. May we all merit hearing the voice of G-d, speaking to us at every moment of the day!

Parashat Bo

In this week's *parashah* the Jewish people received the first mitzvah: "Hashem spoke to Moshe and Aharon in the Land of Egypt, saying, This month shall be to you the beginning of months, it shall be the first month of the year to you" (*Shemot* 12:1–2).

The First Mitzvah of Renewal

The Hebrew word for month *chodesh* also means new. With this first mitzvah to sanctify the new moon, we became renewed as a people. "There is nothing new under the sun" (*Kohelet* 1:9). In the realm of nature (under the sun) life repeats itself along its predestined orbit. Yet, through the *mitzvot* we can connect with the otherworldly reality beyond the sun and the realm of nature. *Sefat Emet* explains that through performing *mitzvot*, we connect with the source of life, which is continual renewal. It is our ability to renew ourselves through the *mitzvot* that makes us Jewish.

By receiving the first mitzvah, the nation of Israel is born. Our sages teach, "A convert who converted is like a baby newly born" (*Yevamot* 62a). It is no wonder then, that the first mitzvah through which we became a Jewish nation is the embodiment of renewal (*chodesh*). Many commentators ask, why the first of the Ten Commandments reads, "I am Hashem your G-d Who has taken you out of Egypt" (*Shemot* 20:2), instead of, "I am Hashem your G-d Who has created you"? When G-d created the world, He created it for the sake of Israel, [imbuing

Israel with the capability to bring all of humanity to perfection] (*Batei Midrashot,* Part 1, *Rabbah d'Bereishit* 4). Since the nation of Israel was born through the Exodus, it becomes indeed the purpose of creation. This is why the first of the Ten Commandments refers to the Exodus rather than to the creation.

In Charge of Nature

It is interesting that we received the mitzvah of sanctifying the new moon which established that Israel is beyond nature, specifically "in the Land of Egypt," which was notorious for worshipping nature. This mitzvah interrupts the Torah's recount of the plague of the firstborn that brought about our redemption. "It shall be the first month of the year to you." The word *lachem* (to you) teaches us that the Jewish people must be personally involved in the process of establishing the beginning of every month. The date of *Rosh Chodesh* (first of the month) was determined by the *beit din* (Jewish court) based on the testimony of eyewitnesses who had actually seen the new moon. Although the wise people of the great *beit din* in Jerusalem knew the astronomical calculations of the calendar, in order that this mitzvah shall be "yours," the declaration of the new month must be verified subjectively as well. Israel's personal involvement in the establishment of the calendar molded the awareness that we are not subordinate to the laws of nature. On the contrary, we are in charge of the times. In order to make this recognition penetrate our awareness, we were handed the responsibility to determine the dates for our holidays. Rabbi S.R. Hirsch points out that if the orbit of the moon automatically had determined the holidays, then the festival of the New Moon would have been a great support for the idol worship of nature. This was the worship of Egypt from which Israel had to urgently be liberated.

To Count from the Month of Our Redemption

According to Ramban, we fulfill the mitzvah to constantly remember the great miracles of the Exodus by enumerating the Hebrew month *Nissan*, the month of redemption as the first month. We lose this opportunity to remember the Exodus when we date our checks 1/23, using number one to refer to the Gregorian month of January. It must be Divine supervision that *Parashat Bo*, which describes the mitzvah to count the month of *Nissan* as the first month of the year, is always read in synagogue during January, the first month of the secular calendar. Could there be a stronger support for Ramban's position never to count any other month than *Nissan* as the first?

Constant Renewal

The rebirth of the moon constantly calls us to become reborn from the nights of routine and corruption. It ensures eternal freshness, to the extent that Israel is forever immune to the spiritual and ethical corruption of Egypt. This Divine clock given to Israel at the verge of redemption is internalized through the experience of womanhood. By means of our monthly cycles, women embody the renewal of the moon. "From my flesh I will see G-d" (*Iyov* 19:26). Through the experience of the changes in our own body, we are able to feel how nothing in life is static. We internalize the realization that life does not run its course automatically like a windup clock. When pregnant or nursing we do not need the monthly cycle to remind us that G-d continues to renew the world. Nothing makes G-d's miraculous renewal of the world clearer than the sensation of a new being growing within us. Moreover, the rapid unfolding of our nursing infant teaches us to keep renewing ourselves as well. By the time of menopause, we will hopefully have integrated the message of the moon into the very fiber of our being.

Seeing Light Within Darkness

The mitzvah of recognizing the new moon takes place in the dark after the sun goes down. Therefore, it was given in Egypt, the place of spiritual darkness. The time of the new moon is connected to the ability to bring light within the dark reality. We do not always feel how the *mitzvot* connect us with the world beyond the sun. One has to be wise in order to see that which is being born (*Pirkei Avot* 2:9). Unless we look very carefully, we will be totally enclosed in the darkness of physical reality. It takes faith to continue to look and anticipate the moment of the moon's rebirth. We need to lift our eyes to the heavens where the silver sliver of the moon is fleeting. Women are known for our faith and ability to see beyond our immediate reality. Our nurturing role allows us to visualize the fulfillment of the potential of our loved ones, and gives us faith that our giving eventually will bear fruit. "The woman was given more *binah* than the man" (*Bereishit Rabbah* 18:1). The word *binah* means both intuition and building. A woman has the ability to build a tiny seed into a fully developed baby. Just as the newborn moon waxes and becomes full, the baby develops and grows within the womb.

G-d began the inner molding of His people by establishing the renewal of the moon as a sign that would repeat itself throughout the year. In this way the experience of self-renewal would be engraved within our hearts. Thus, the mitzvah of sanctifying the new moon gives us the ability to guard the feeling of excitement for the future time of redemption. The light of freedom that first rose in the horizon of the lives of the Jews during the Exodus and opened up new heavens before them continues to glow today. Its radiance will be renewed multifold at the time of our final redemption.

Parashat Beshalach

The Torah describes the song of Miriam and the women after the song of Moshe and the men at the sea: "Miriam the prophetess, Aharon's sister, took the drum in her hand, and all the women went after her with drums and dances" (*Shemot* 15:20).

The Song of the Women at the Sea

Why did the Torah repeat the entire first verse of the Song of the Sea when describing the song of Miriam and the women who joined her? Malbim explains that the women's song is mentioned separately to emphasize that the Exodus took place in their merit. The women of that generation, therefore, received their own prophecy at the sea.

Miriam the Prophetess

The Torah calls Miriam "the prophetess" at the splitting of the sea and the Talmud enumerates her as one of the seven prophetesses:

> *Miriam prophesied that her mother would give birth to a son who would redeem Israel. When Moshe was born and the house was filled with light, her father got up, kissed her and said, "My daughter, your prophecy has been fulfilled." When they put him in the Nile, her father rose, struck her head and asked, "My daughter, what will become of your prophecy?" Therefore, it states, "His sister stood from afar"* (*Shemot* 2:4) *to find out what would be the end of her prophecy* (*Megillah* 14a).

According to the Talmud, it is not clear why Miriam was called a prophetess at the sea rather than prior to the birth of Moshe, when she originally prophesied. *Etz Yosef* explains that only at the culmination of the Exodus did Miriam's prophecy become totally fulfilled. Rabbeinu Bachaya notes that Miriam is the first person to be named a prophet in the Torah. The first time the Torah mentions the word "prophet" is in regards to a woman, in order to emphasize the great level that women attained at the sea, as it states: "A maidservant at the sea saw more than even Yechezkel ben Buzi" (*Mechilta, Beshalach* 3). *Kli Yakar* agrees that Miriam became a prophetess at the splitting of the sea, since the women merited seeing the *Shechinah* at that time. They played drums and danced in order to draw down the spirit of prophecy, as the Divine Presence only rests upon us when we are filled with happiness (*Shabbat* 30b).

Rabbeinu Bachaya concludes that important matters in the Torah are often expressed through women. For example, the concept of the World to Come is called "a bundle of life" by Avigail, wife of David (1 *Shemuel* 25:29). Channah, the Mother of our Prayer, taught the concept of the revival of the dead (1 *Shemuel* 2:6), and the order of prayer. Reincarnation is alluded to by the wise woman from Tekoah (2 *Shemuel* 14:14). All these instances show the importance of the role of women in the Torah.

Women and Drums in the Wilderness

"All the women went after her with drums and dances." How did the women have drums in the wilderness? The righteous women in that generation were confident that Hashem would perform great miracles at the Exodus, and they accordingly had brought drums with them from Egypt (Rashi, *Shemot* 15:20). Why is bringing drums from Egypt such an act of righteousness?

Let us imagine the scene of the Exodus. For the past three generations, Egypt has served as the home of the Jews. Their belongings have accumulated. Most of their possessions will have to be left behind, since they are rushing out on such short notice, without even sufficient time to let their bread rise. They are leaving only with what can fit on the backs of their donkeys. Generally, when a woman packs for a prolonged journey, she needs to consider food, clothing, various utensils, sleepwear, etc. In a high pressure situation like that of the Exodus, when there is barely enough time for the essentials, it is likely that spirituality and the need to praise G-d will be pushed aside. The greatness of the Jewish women in Egypt was their realization that there was nothing more essential than bringing G-d into the picture. Likewise, unless we make G-d the center of our lives, nothing else has any purpose.

Faith and Praise

Most people seek out G-d only when in great danger or when they are going through hard times. The Jewish women in Egypt knew how to connect to Hashem and praise Him during happy times as well. Although it is natural to notice the negative and fear the unknown, the Jewish women in Egypt praised Hashem not only for His present deliverance, but also for His future salvation, which they envisioned. Unlike the men, who greatly feared Pharaoh's approaching army, the women were steadfast in their faith, overcoming the elements of haste, pressure, and peril. While the men complained to Moshe asking, "...are there not enough graves in Egypt that you have taken us to die in the wilderness?" (*Shemot* 14:11), the women confidently believed in G-d's miraculous upcoming liberation. When they escaped from Egypt, they packed not only the essentials for physical survival, but had their spiritual instruments at hand – the drums that they would use to praise Hashem for miracles to come.

The Song of Miracles and Forgiveness

The word for dances in Hebrew is *mecholot*. This word also means forgiveness. The Midrash concludes that whoever praises G-d in song for a miracle performed for him becomes a new creation with all his sins forgiven (*Yalkut Shimoni, Shemot* 15:254). Rabbi Simcha Zissel explains that the Torah repeats an entire verse when describing Miriam's song, since there could be no deeper understanding than that of the Jews at the sea. When Miriam repeated, "Let us sing to Hashem" (*Shemot* 15:21), she was imbued with the depth of a new realization. Therefore, it is considered as if she created a completely new song. The drumming and dancing of all the women became sanctified, and every word in the verses of their song was renewed. From this we learn that when our actions are permeated with strong feeling, understanding, complete faith and deep intention, they have the ability to transform and renew the old. Along the same lines, we celebrate Shabbat, Pesach and Sukkot in order to internalize how G-d changed the order of creation at the Exodus, and renew our understanding and faith in Hashem, the Creator and ruler of the world. Singing is more than just reading or speaking an idea. When a person bursts into song, she can internalize an intellectual concept, connect it to her feelings and integrate it deep within the faculties of her entire being. By praising Hashem through song, we understand G-d's greatness from a novel perspective, and renew our relationship with the Divine. This process of complete renewal within our mind and emotions transforms us into a new being whose previous sins are forgiven.

Parashat Yitro

"Moshe went up to G-d, and Hashem called to him out of the mountain saying, Thus shall you say (*tomar*) to the house of Ya'acov, and tell (*tagid*) the sons of Israel" (*Shemot* 19:3).

Chief of Her Home

Rashi explains that "the house of Ya'acov" refers to the women – to them you shall speak in gentle language, as the Hebrew word *tomar* (say) indicates. "To the sons of Israel" – the men, Moshe is instructed to communicate the punishments and details of the commandments in words "as hard as wormwood," implied by the Hebrew word, *tagid* (tell). According to *Sha'arei Aharon*, "the house of Ya'acov" refers to the woman, because she is the chief of her home (*akeret habayit*). The Hebrew term *akeret habayit* has been translated as "housewife." However, a preferred translation might be "homemaker," an appellation more congruent with the original Hebrew term that is intended as a title of honor. Western culture misleads us into believing that a woman obtains her primary fulfillment outside the home, and needs only to take care of domestic chores on the side.

The following anecdote serves to demonstrate the absurdity of this outlook: A certain executive once asked his fellow associate what his wife does. The associate responded, "She is in charge of a home for unwanted children." This sounded like a position of prestige, until it became clear that the children that she was in charge of were her own!

We need to reeducate ourselves to appreciate the importance of the title: *akeret habayit*. What could be more important than setting the tone in the home for all future generations?

Women and Matan Torah

Rabbeinu Bachaya explains that the reason the Torah was given to the woman first was because of her role as the one who imbues the home with Torah values; guiding the children in the ways of Torah. Therefore, the perpetuation of the Torah for all future generations depends upon the woman.

Women are Motivated by Love

According to *Be'er Yitzchak*, Moshe was instructed to tell the women only about their important mission and the reward of keeping the *mitzvot*. From hearing the positive, they would be able to deduce the opposite. The men, however, needed a detailed explanation of the punishments for transgressing the commandments. From this, we may infer that one major difference between men and women is that women are predominantly motivated by love, while men by fear. Moreover, men need to be told directly whereas women have the ability to read between the lines and understand allusions. This superior level of intuition and softness of heart are part of our unique feminine assets that need to be cultivated rather than renounced.

Women as Initiators

The Midrash gives several reasons why Hashem gave the Torah to the woman first. At creation, G-d only commanded Adam not to eat from the Tree of Knowledge. Chava was not commanded directly by G-d, and this was a major reason why she was vulnerable to succumb to the snake's temptation to eat from the Tree and share its fruit with her husband. Therefore, in order to assure that the women would keep the Torah, G-d decided to give the Torah to the women first. Another reason is because women are eager to keep the *mitzvot*, and moreover, because they will ensure that their children keep the Torah (*Shemot Rabbah* 28:2). *Maharsha* explains that the word *tagid* can grammatically be read, "she shall tell." Our verse can, therefore, be explained as follows, "Thus shall you say to the woman, that **she shall tell** the sons of Israel." We often find that women have the power of persuasion, and ability to influence others. This point is illustrated by the following anecdote: A pious man was married to a pious woman. Since they had no children for more than ten years, they decided to divorce. When the pious man married a wicked woman, she influenced him to become wicked as well. However, the pious woman was able to make a righteous person out of the wicked man she had married. From this we learn that everything derives from the woman (*Bereishit Rabbah* 17:2). The Torah was given to the woman first, because when she understands the importance of the Torah, she will ensure that everyone around her understands it as well. Just like it is the woman who gives birth physically, so does she bring forth spirituality and Torah into the world.

Parashat Mishpatim

"If a man sells his daughter to be a maidservant..." (*Shemot* 21:7). The laws of Jewish slaves are difficult to deal with, especially for women. We wonder how it can be fair that a father has the right to sell his daughter to become a maidservant. Which transgression made her deserve such a degrading position? It is, however, an unfortunate fact of life, that the social position of parents often affects their children.

The Hebrew Maidservant

Ralbag explains that a man is not allowed to sell his daughter unless he has absolutely no other way to support himself. Rambam concurs that the father may only sell his daughter, in case he becomes so destitute that he loses all his possessions including the shirt off his back. Although he sold her because of destitution, the father should be forced to redeem her, and avoid a blemish on the family. According to Rashi, the father dealt deceitfully with her by selling her to a man who was unwilling to marry her when she reached maturity. Her father would, therefore, not be permitted to sell her again. This is alluded to in the end of the following verse, "...seeing that he has dealt deceitfully with her" (*Shemot* 21:8), which according to the simple meaning refers to the master who neglected his moral obligation to marry his maidservant. Rashi adds that "he" could also refer to the father. *Me'Am Lo'ez* agrees and explains that the father behaved in an extremely cruel way. He should rather have become a stone carrier to avoid selling his own daughter. The *Minchah Belulah* notes that our verse calls the father "a man" because he does not deserve the title "father," since he had no mercy on his daughter. He treated her as a stranger, contrary to what is expected of a father.

A Protection for the Daughter

If selling one's daughter as a maidservant is such an act of cruelty, then why does the Torah permit it in the first place? Perhaps the laws of the maidservant are intended to protect the daughter. When a father is not in a position to support her, he has the opportunity to hand over her care to someone who will provide for her. The laws of slaves ensure that the master treats her exactly as his own daughter, providing her with the same standard of beds, clothing and food. The master is also not allowed to make her do degrading kinds of work such as tying his shoes. When she reaches maturity, the man who took her in as a maidservant is expected to either marry her himself or marry her off to his son. Upon marriage, the Torah makes clear that she receives the exact same rights as a free woman: "If he has betrothed her unto his son, he shall do unto her after the manner of daughters" (*Shemot* 21:9). Let us imagine what would happen in Biblical times to a poor girl without this social institution. She might die of starvation, or have to degrade herself searching through garbage for potato peels. Who would ever want to marry this sullen eyed girl in rags, without a dowry? Becoming a maidservant protected her from having to sleep on hard straw mats and washing toilet seats until the end of her life.

The Duties of the Husband

"If he takes another wife; her food (*she'erah*), her clothing, and her conjugal rights he shall not diminish" (*Shemot* 21:10). Rashi explains that this verse refers to the son who has agreed to marry his father's maidservant. If he takes a free woman as an additional wife, he is not allowed to diminish the marital rights of the former maidservant. The word *she'erah* which Rashi translates as food, literally means flesh. The reason it is called *she'erah* according to Ibn Ezra, is that the food maintains the flesh of the body. This verse is the source of the Torah obligation that a man must provide his wife with food, clothing and conjugal rights. Ramban, however, disagrees and insists that had Scripture intended food, it would have used the word *lechem* – bread, which is the usual way of referring to food. Therefore, he holds that the obligation of the husband to provide sustenance for his wife is only rabbinical. The word *she'erah* refers instead, according to Ramban, to closeness of the flesh. This implies that a man is not allowed to treat his wife in the way of the Persians, who live together, while being fully dressed. The Jewish way of intimacy involves closeness of bodies without the interference of clothes.

The Maidservant's Equal Status

Rabbi S.R. Hirsch notes that the only place in which the Torah mentions the obligations of a husband towards his wife is regarding the maidservant. The Torah purposely defines the elementary rights of Jewish wives through the example of a woman from the lowest rung, the child of a beggar compelled to sell his daughter as a slave to save her from starvation. The maidservant, disdainfully refused by her master now becomes the wife of his son. When she is placed beside an ordinary bride, a girl married out of a free rich family, the Torah proclaims: "Not by one hair's breadth may the treatment of the one differ from that given to the other." The Torah singles out this case as an example of the general rights of married women in order to teach the following principle: "With marriage a woman rises to her husband's station in life, but never falls from hers." Whether she brought a dowry of gold and silver, or came to him as the tattered naked child of a beggar, she has the right to be treated according to his station in life. She is treated even higher, if she was used to a higher standard of living than her husband.

Marital Intimacy – The Right of a Wife

Having intimacy with her husband is the right of every wife. According to Rambam a man who marries a Jewish woman is prohibited from causing his wife pain by withholding any of her three basic rights. The *Shulchan Aruch* teaches that if a husband withholds physical intimacy from his wife, he transgresses the Torah injunction: "her conjugal rights he shall not diminish." (*Even HaEzer* 76:11). *Be'er Heitiv* comments that if he doesn't intend to hurt her, but his business trips prevent him from having intimacy with her according to the prescribed times, he is not transgressing the Torah injunction. The reason is that most women are willing to wait longer to be with their husband, when they are compensated by the extra profit he brings home. Alshech, however, holds that even when the husband does not purposely withhold the conjugal rights of his wife, he still transgresses Torah law.

In our modern society, sex is usually regarded as something the woman gives to her man. The fact that marital intimacy is the right of the wife and not vice versa, teaches us an important principle about the Torah's attitude towards physical relationships. Although the man may have a greater sexual desire, living with his wife should be an unselfish act of giving in order to satisfy her need. Most women do not detach sexuality from emotional and spiritual closeness. This is why women rarely use harlots. By commanding the man to direct his sexuality towards satisfying the desire of his wife, the Torah ensures that intimacy between husband and wife reaches beyond the physical. Only when the woman holds the key to marital intimacy, can the holy union between husband and wife encompass all levels of reality, including the physical, emotional, and spiritual.

Parashat Terumah

"Let them make me a sanctuary that I may dwell within them" (*Shemot* 25:8). Since the six hundred and thirteen *mitzvot* are eternal, there has to be a way to keep them at any given time. How is it then possible to fulfill the mitzvah of building the Temple in our time?

A Personal Sanctuary

Rabbi Ya'acov Yosef from Polnoye answers that since every person is a small world, each of us can build a sanctuary within our heart for the Divine Presence to dwell. In this way the continuation of the verse can be fulfilled, "that I may dwell within them." If our heart can become the dwelling place for the Divine Presence, certainly the Jewish home can be compared to the Temple, as it is known that a Jewish home is called a *mikdash me'at* (a miniature sanctuary).

The Jewish Home – A Miniature Sanctuary

Being the chief of her home, the woman is compared to the *Kohen Gadol* (High Priest) and her housework to his Divine service. Just as the *Kohen Gadol* kindles the *menorah* (candelabra) in *Beit HaMikdash* (the Temple), the woman lights the Shabbat candles in her home. The bread she bakes is like the showbread in the Temple. The food she cooks is like a *korban* (sacrifice), and the table she sets is a *mizbeach* (altar). Her goal is to imbue her home with spirituality and fear of G-d. In the same manner that the *Kohen Gadol* causes the *Shechinah* to dwell in the world, the woman invites the *Shechinah* to enter her home. Just like the *Kohen Gadol* is not inferior to the king, so is the wife not inferior to her husband. They complete one another, each performing their vital function.

Like the Tent of Sarah

In *Parashat Chayei Sarah* we learned that Yitzchak brought Rivkah into his mother, Sarah's tent (*Bereishit* 24:67). Rashi explains that the tent of Sarah was unique in three ways. While Sarah was living, a light had been burning in the tent from one Shabbat eve to the next. There was a continuous blessing in the dough, and the Cloud of Glory was always hanging over the tent. However, since her death, all of this had stopped. When Rivkah entered, these three blessings reappeared. Thus, we see that the *Mishkan* is modeled after the home of Sarah *Imainu* (our mother). The eternal light of the *menorah* corresponds to the light burning in her tent, and the showbread that would stay warm and fresh from one Shabbat eve to the next is compared to the blessing in her dough. The Cloud of Glory hanging over Sarah's tent is the same cloud that "…covered the appointed tent…" and filled the Tabernacle with Hashem's glory (*Shemot* 40:34). These special qualities of the Jewish home were inherited by Rivkah. She transmitted them to the chain of future Jewish women. We are the receivers of these spiritual genetics that enable us to enter the tent of Sarah and transform our home into a dwelling place for G-d's Feminine Indwelling Presence (*Shechinah*).

The Virtues of a Jewish Woman

The Maharal explains that a Jewish woman merits the blessings of Sarah's tent through her performance of the special *mitzvot* designated for women. The *bracha* in the dough corresponds to the mitzvah of taking *challah* (bread offering), and the burning light corresponds to the mitzvah of lighting the Shabbat candles. The cloud hanging over her tent is the cloud of Hashem's *Shechinah* that a woman merits by keeping the mitzvah of *taharat hamishpachah* (family purity), because purity (*taharah*) leads to holiness (*Gur Aryeh, Bereishit* 24:67). In addition to being in the merit of performing the special *mitzvot* designated for women, these blessings teach us the virtues that every Jewish woman should aspire to achieve. Being intelligent causes the Cloud of the Divine Presence and prophecy to rest upon her. The blessing in the dough occurs when a woman takes care of the needs of her home and watches over its belongings. Remaining calm and peaceful, avoiding fights and tension causes the candle, a symbol of peace, to burn infinitely. The light of the candle is also a symbol of Torah learning, as it states: "For the mitzvah is a candle, and Torah is light" (*Mishlei* 6:23). Therefore, when we light the Shabbat candles, it is a custom to pray for children, who will illuminate the world with their Torah (*Yafet Toar* on *Bereishit Rabbah* 60:16).

Baby Faced Cherubs

"You shall make two cherubs of gold" (*Shemot* 25:18). The cherubs symbolize our young children, as Rashi explains, "...they had the form of a child's face." Just like the cherubs were attached to the Holy Ark containing the Tablets of the Law, so must we ensure that our little ones are educated to attach themselves to Torah. Rabbi Meir Shapira explains that the utensils of the sanctuary could be made from any metal, if there was no gold to be found. The cherubs, however, had to be made from pure gold. This teaches us that when it comes to a matter as important as child education, no compromise is acceptable. We are obligated to give them the very best, as their Torah learning is worth much more than gold.

Parashat Tetzaveh

This week's *parashah* gives a detailed description of the *Kohanim's* garments. Each garment with its deep symbolic significance must also be exquisite and splendid in appearance. "You shall make garments of holiness for Aharon your brother for glory and for splendor" (*Shemot* 28:2). Rabbi S.R. Hirsch explains that whereas the word glory expresses the spiritual and ethical virtue of the *Kehunah*, the word splendor adds the element of beauty. Thus, it is clear that according to the Torah a dignified outward appearance goes hand in hand with inner spiritual attainment.

Must We Be Well Dressed?

In his description of the Woman of Valor, King Shlomo, likewise, highlights the importance of being well dressed: "Luxurious bedspreads she made herself, fine linen (*shes*) and purple (*argaman*) are her clothing" (*Mishlei* 31:22). It is interesting to note that fine linen and purple (*shes v'argaman*) are the same materials used for the garments of the *Kohanim*: "They shall take the gold, and the blue purple, and the red purple, (*argaman*) and the crimson, and the fine linen (*shes*)" (*Shemot* 28:5). Thus, our comparison between the Woman of Valor and the *Kohen Gadol* from *Parashat Terumah* (on page 69) can be extended to comprise not only her home and work, but her clothing as well. This is, moreover, alluded to in the verse which reads, "She seeks wool and linen" (*Mishlei* 31:13), since only the *Kohen Gadol* is permitted to wear a mixture of these materials. (The garments of the *Kohen Gadol* are excempted from the prohibition to wear a mixture of wool and linen called *shatnes*). Just as the *Kohanim* are commanded to dress "for glory and for splendor," it is not becoming for a woman to neglect herself like a self-sacrificing *shemata* (doormat) dressed in shapeless hand-me-downs. The woman of valor understands the importance of dressing in a dignified manner.

G-d's Ambassador in the World

I have often been confronted with the following question: "How come a religious woman is allowed to wear a wig that is more beautiful than her own hair?" Some people confuse the notion that a Jewish woman must dress modestly, and think that she is obligated to make herself unattractive. The purpose of wearing modest garments is not to make oneself look ugly. Actually, many people look better dressed than undressed. This does not make them more modest without clothes! I am not trying to defend the custom of wearing wigs. I myself prefer the freer flowing, practical look of the headscarf. However, arguing that wigs might make a woman look more beautiful is invalid, since the purpose of dressing modestly is not to make oneself look horrible. When I was once interviewed for a newspaper, the journalist expressed his surprise that I was wearing eye makeup: "I thought married women must cover their hair in order to look unattractive to other men, so how come you are allowed to wear makeup?" I explained that according to the Torah we are created in the image of G-d. Therefore, we must dress accordingly. As a Jew I am a representative of G-d in the world, in the same manner that an ambassador represents his country abroad. Just like my actions ought to be immaculate, so too must my outward appearance be attractive to reflect my Creator – the Master of the Universe. I might have phrased my thoughts differently had I known that my picture would later appear with the caption, "I am G-d's ambassador."

Is Beauty Vain?

"Grace is false, and beauty is vain, a woman who fears G-d, she shall be praised" (*Mishlei* 31:30). From this verse, it sounds as though outward beauty must be avoided, since it is called false and vain. However, the *Kohanim* are commanded to wear garments "for glory and for splendor." Likewise, the Woman of Valor is praised for wearing "fine linen and purple," and for being dressed in majesty. Outward beauty, therefore, cannot be opposed to fear of G-d. Beauty is only false and vain when we strive towards it for its own sake. We must not be blinded by the flashiness of outward beauty and forget that the main goal is to attain true fear of G-d. Being well dressed is a means to serve G-d in a more refined way. We do not beautify ourselves for our own self-aggrandizement; rather, our intention must be to honor G-d by being crowned in beauty. In this way the Jewish woman becomes like the *Kohen*, whose dress code is a reflection of the way he honors G-d.

Parashat Ki Tisa

"Aharon said unto them; take off the golden earrings which are in your wives' ears…" (*Shemot* 32:2). Rashi explains that Aharon had in mind to postpone making the Golden Calf, since he knew that women would not easily part with their jewelry. He hoped that Moshe would arrive in the meantime.

Women Refused to Make the Golden Calf

Since the women did not want to donate their jewelry to the Golden Calf, the men took off their own golden earrings instead. This is understood from the following verse: "All the people pulled off the golden pendants that were in their ears, and brought them to Aharon" (*Shemot* 32:3). The word *ozneihem* (their ears) is written in the masculine form suggesting the fact that the men pulled off their own earrings, without any reference to the pendants belonging to the women. *Minchah Belulah* is of the opinion that the men pulled off their wives' earrings by force. In either case, the women refused to participate in making the Golden Calf.

To Be Renewed Like the Moon

When the wives refused to hand over earrings to their husbands, they told them, "We will not listen to you and make a disgusting thing, which has no power." For this, G-d rewarded them in this world by giving them the primary responsibility to celebrate *Rosh Chodesh* (the

Festival of the New Moon) over the men. Hashem also gave them the reward in the World to Come, to be renewed like the moon (*Pirkei d'Rabbi Eliezer* 44). The *Tur* explains why celebrating *Rosh Chodesh* was a suitable reward for the women for not participating in the Golden Calf. The three pilgrim festivals correspond to Avraham, Yitzchak and Ya'acov, whereas, *Rosh Chodesh* corresponded to the twelve tribes. When the tribes sinned by making the Golden Calf, *Rosh Chodesh* was taken away from them and given to their wives. There are different opinions as to the extent that women should refrain from work to celebrate *Rosh Chodesh*, and as to whether this is an optional custom or a halachic obligation. The *Beur Halachah* concludes that it is the general consensus that women must refrain from some kind of work, in particular heavy work, in order to make the day special and different.

The Golden Calf – A Tangible Object

According to Yehudah HaLevi the sin of the Golden Calf was not idol worship, but rather the manifestation of a desire to serve G-d by tangible means. For the nations of that era, physical forms and symbols functioned as focal points for prayer and meditation. The Israelite masses hoped that Moshe would bring down something concrete from heaven to which they could direct their hearts and thought the Tablets were intended to serve this purpose (*The Kuzari* 1:37). They lacked the complete understanding that the Almighty, Who is in charge of nature and everything within it, can never be contained within a physical object.

Rosh Chodesh – Eternal Renewal

What is the underlying connection between the refusal to give earrings for the Golden Calf and the specific reward of celebrating *Rosh Chodesh*? The mitzvah of sanctifying the new moon was given to Israel at the verge of the Exodus, in order to teach Israel to break with the Egyptian mentality of idolizing nature. The moon wanes and waxes, and therefore, cannot be confined to any fixed form. We were handed the responsibility to determine the date of *Rosh Chodesh* by means of witnesses, to teach us how nature has no independent power, but rather is subordinate to the consciousness of the person performing a mitzvah. The fact that *Rosh Chodesh* is not predetermined by fixed calculations ensures eternal renewal, contrary to the Egyptian outlook preoccupied with death and stagnation.

Women and Moon Consciousness

When the women refused to give their jewelry to the Golden Calf, they confirmed the lesson of the new moon. While the men were hanging on to the old ways, and desired something concrete to rely on, the women were ready for the spiritual renewal of Divine commandments embodied in the mitzvah to sanctify the new moon. They understood that in the same way that the new moon cannot be contained within a fixed date, so too G-d cannot be contained within any bounds, as He is the life force that renews everything in nature. Even the physical appearance of the moon testifies to its dynamic message. Perhaps it is easier for women to tune into this "moon consciousness" of flexibility because our role as caretakers does not always result in tangible rewards. Our children train us to act with patience – a quality that the men at Sinai lacked. Their impatience in waiting for Moshe made them decide to construct a replacement.

Golden Earrings and Slave Mentality

Sha'arei Aharon brings in the name of Ariza"l, that a Torah scholar may be dominated by his wife because in an earlier reincarnation he did not stop the vast multitude from making the Golden Calf. From all the golden jewelry owned by the Jewish people, the Torah specifically emphasizes earrings in connection with making the Golden Calf. This reminds us of the law regarding the Jewish slave who refuses to go free. His ear is pierced and he must serve until all the slaves go free at the end of the jubilee cycle (*Shemot* 21:6). Rashi asks why the ear had to be pierced rather than any other limb of the servant's body. He answers, "The ear which heard G-d say on Mount Sinai, 'For unto Me the children of Israel are servants' (*Vayikra* 25:55), yet its owner went and procured for himself another master – let it be pierced." The earring worn in the pierced ear symbolizes an inability to serve G-d directly.

The slave who exchanged the Holy Master with a mortal master, is unable to surrender completely to G-d, but requires an intermediary between himself and his Eternal Master. From the fact that the men at Sinai wore earrings like the Egyptian men, we learn that they had not detached themselves completely from the slave mentality of Egypt.

The Golden Calf was supposed to be a replacement for Moshe, as it states: "…arise, make us gods, which shall go before us; for this Moshe, the man that brought us out of the Land of Egypt, we do not know what has become of him" (*Shemot* 32:1). Thus, the men at Sinai can be compared to the slave who clings to his mortal master. The women were more independent. Although a *kosher* wife acts according to the will of her husband (*Yalkut Shimoni*, *Shoftim* 4:42), the women at Sinai understood that this only applies as long as it brings us closer to G-d. The men needed a leader they could blindly obey, whereas the women did not need an intermediary, for they were directly in tune with the eternal will of G-d.

Parashat Vayakhel

"They came, both men and women, as many as were willing hearted, and brought clasps, and pendants, rings and golden beads, all vessels of gold" (*Shemot* 35:22). The expression translated in our verse as "both men and women" reads in the Hebrew, *ha'anashim al hanashim* which literally means "the men **on** the women." Rashi, Ramban and Rabbeinu Bachaya explain that the women took off their jewelry and brought it at once. They preceded the men in bringing clasps, pendants, rings, golden beads and different vessels of gold.

For the Mishkan, the Women Gave First

When the men arrived they found that the women had already brought their contribution. This is a great tribute to the women, who had previously refused to give anything to the Golden Calf. The above explanation would also hold true had the verse read *ha'anashim acharei hanashim* – "the men **after** the women." Perhaps the word *al* which literally means **on** alludes to the fact that in preparing for the *Mishkan*, the men relied **on** the women. It was the merit of the righteous women that enabled the building of the *Mishkan*. G-d rewarded the women both in this world and in the coming world for refusing to give to their jewelry to the Golden Calf, yet giving generously to the *Mishkan*, which was erected on *Rosh Chodesh*. They received the privilege to keep *Rosh Chodesh* more than the men in this world, and they will be rewarded in the coming world to be renewed like the moon

(*Pirkei d'Rabbi Eliezer* 44). May the renewal of the wisdom of women bring about the building of the Temple in our time!

To Give Or Not to Give

The greatness of the women who refused to participate in making the Golden Calf is proven by their eagerness to give their gold to the building of the *Mishkan*. Had their generous spirit not prompted them to jump at the opportunity to donate their jewelry for a good cause, one could have suspected that they withheld their jewelry from the Golden Calf because they were stingy, and wanted to keep their gold for themselves. The women at Sinai teach us the importance of knowing when to give and when not to give. Certain people give indiscriminately without knowing whether their gift can be misused or even used against them. Others frantically hold on to their possessions, not realizing that what we give comes back to us, and neither silver nor gold can be taken to the grave. It is a challenge to develop the right balance of giving. We need to use our feminine intuition to discern when and how to give in a way that truly benefits the recipient.

Through the Work of Their Hands

"All the women that were wise hearted did spin with their hands, and brought what they had spun, both of sky-blue and purple, and scarlet and fine linen. And all the women whose heart prompted them in wisdom spun goats' hair" (*Shemot* 35:25–26). Why does it state "spin with their hands"? Is it possible to spin without the hands? There are certain women who are able to teach others to spin while lacking skills in the use of their own hands. Therefore, it states, "with their hands," to show that they were not only wise, but knew how to use their hands as well. They did not hire workers to do the spinning for them, but put their own effort into the spinning, out of love for the mitzvah. This is contrasted to the men who only brought readymade materials as it states: "Every man, with whom was found sky-blue, purple, scarlet and fine linen etc." (*Shemot* 35:23). Therefore, the Torah emphasizes that the women were different. Each woman spun the material with her own hands, according to the wisdom of her heart.

In our modern society, where everything can be bought ready-made, we often lose contact with the satisfaction of expressing our creativity through the loving gifts of handicraft. How much love and devotion goes into the hand knitted sweater that grandma is dedicating to her new grandchild! The image of her loved one is on her mind with each purl and knit. How sweet is the scent of homemade *challah* emerging from our kitchens on the eve of Shabbat, as well as the sight of matching Shabbat dresses sewn lovingly by the mother. When my son voiced his well-meaning praise of my homemade ice-cream, "It is almost as good as store bought," I knew something had gone wrong in our consumer society. The puffed up attractiveness of uniform machine made goodies that fill the shelves of our supermarkets have made us forget to value the importance of the individual talent and creativity of womanhood.

Women, Creativity, and Divine Assistance

While reading this, you might object that you just don't know how to weave, spin, or bake so you have no choice but to buy things ready-made. Yet, the women in the wilderness teach us not to despair. Where there is a will there is a way. This is alluded to by the grammatical difficulty in our verse, "Every woman that was wise hearted did spin with their hands." The tense of the verb does not fit the subject. Whereas, the subject is written in singular, *kol isha* (every woman), the verb is written in plural, *tavu* (they spun). The *Shach* explains that as soon as the women would take the sky-blue wool to spin, Divine assistance caused it to be spun by itself. Therefore, the word for spin (*tavu*) is written in the plural, since Hashem would spin together with them. Likewise, women of today do not need to despair of ever being able to express our individual creativity. When excitement and artistic devotion spurs us on to paint, sew, knit, bake, weave or spin, G-d will surely assist our loving endeavor.

From Off the Backs of the Goats

"All the women that were **wise** hearted…And all the women whose heart prompted them in **wisdom**…" Why is the word "wisdom" used in connection with the women who spun the goats' hair? This indicates that spinning the goats' hair required additional wisdom apart from spinning the sky-blue, purple and scarlet threads. Because our verse reads, *tavu et haizim,* literally, "spun the goats," Rashi explains that the women had the extraordinary skill of spinning directly from off the backs of the goats. The reason behind this unusual skill was the desire of all the women to participate in the work of the *Mishkan,* even those who were *niddah* (separated) and therefore unable to engage in the general work of the *Mishkan.* These women would spin from off the back of the goats, because the animals do not receive *tumah* (ritual impurity). In addition, certain wise women chose specifically to to be involved with the spinning the goats' hair, while the rest of the women were busy preparing the materials needed for the magnificent curtains of the *Mishkan*. Although, the former occupation was less glorious, it was more vital for the protection of the *Mishkan*, because it constituted the main part of the tent as taught by Rabbi S.R. Hirsch. Moreover, the essence of womanhood is manifest in the concept of the tent. By choosing the vital over the attractive, and identifying with the main part of the tent, these women expressed the wisdom and power of womanhood.

Parashat Pekudei

Parashat Pekudei is often neglected. Usually, it is joined to *Parashat Vayakhel*, and seems to be hiding behind it. Yet, every Torah reading has equal importance, since every word of the Torah comprises the word of the living G-d.

Behind the Facade

In order to understand the importance and spiritual message of *Parashat Pekudei*, we need to look deeper. This can be compared to the relationship between a husband and wife. Although the wife may appear to be standing in the shade of her husband, this does not indicate that she has less value. As we explained in *Parashat Bereishit*, both are equally created in the image of G-d. "Behind every great man is a great woman." If we are to understand the spiritual impact of the Jewish woman, we need to look deeper, behind the facade.

Connecting the Spiritual with the Mundane

"All the gold that was applied for the work in all the work of the holy place, the gold of the offering, was twenty-nine talents, and seven hundred and thirty shekels, in the holy shekel" (*Shemot* 38:24). One can only wonder why the book of *Shemot*, which is called "The Book of Redemption," culminates in a mere accounting of materials, rather than ending on a grand spiritual note. This teaches us an important principle in Judaism. Unlike certain religions, Judaism is not just a spiritual ideology disconnected from the world, but a practical way of life as well. We are not commanded to separate ourselves from the world while meditating on Hashem's name. If that were the purpose of the Torah, it would have been given to the angels, who have no part in this physical world. Our purpose, however, is to build a dwelling place for Hashem below by carrying out the spiritual message of the Torah, and applying it to day-to-day concerns. It is our task to forge a connection between the Torah and even the most mundane business. The culmination of the Exodus is not simply receiving the Torah, but being able to apply it to material circumstances, such as monetary matters. Similarly, it is the challenge of the Jewish women to connect our mundane tasks of career and homemaking with the spirit of building a dwelling place for G-d below.

Holding the Jewish People Together

"Of the thousand seven hundred and seventy-five shekels he made hooks for the pillars" (*Shemot* 38:28). A hook is called a *vav* in Hebrew. The letter *vav*, when used as *vav hachibur* (the connecting *vav*), also means "and." This *vav* according to Kabbalah is the letter of truth (*Zohar,* part 3, 2b.) The second set of Torah Tablets was never broken because the Ten Commandments were connected with this *vav*. The importance of *vav hachibur* is also illustrated by the connection between the book of *Shemot*, which ends with *Parashat Pekudei* and the book of *Vayikra*, which starts with the letter *vav*. Although the golden *menorah* and the ark with its cherubs are glamorous, we must not forget the seemingly insignificant hooks, clasps, and pegs which connected the entire *Mishkan*, without them everything would fall apart. Women have a role similar to these hooks. Our purpose may not be as upfront as that of men, yet we are as indispensable as the hooks of the *Mishkan*, in our ability to hold the Jewish people together.

The Mother is the Condition of Existence

The word for mother in Hebrew is *eim* which also means "if" – the necessary condition enabling something else to exist. Mothers are the condition upon which the Jewish people depend. Not surprisingly, a person's Jewishness depends on the status of his or her mother. The word *emunah* is also linked to the word *eim* and enables the tradition to be passed throughout the generations. Being the main link in all of these ways, the mother has a major influence in determining the extent to which her children will absorb the Torah way of living. Therefore, the physical and spiritual future of the next generation depends on the mothers.

A Mother's Flexibility

One difference between the Golden Calf and the *Mishkan* is the *Mishkan*'s ability to be taken apart and joined together anew. The Golden Calf, on the other hand, turned to dust and ashes when broken down. A link that is meant to be eternal must possess the flexibility to be rejoined after coming apart. This ability symbolizes our willingness to start anew. If we think we understand something just because we have learned it once, we are mistaken. To really understand a matter requires being able to take it apart and put it together again. This flexibility is an essential quality of womanhood. As soon as we have finished mopping the floor, someone walks in, with mud on the shoes, and we have to start all over. Not long after taking the cake out of the oven, is it eaten, and we get the flour and eggs ready again. As mothers, we must be flexible to allow our chores to be constantly interrupted by the urgent cry of the baby. We must be willing to keep starting anew, as our work is constantly undone.

The Hooks of Creation

The *Mishkan* corresponds to the work of creation. The greatest wonders of everything in creation are the joints. The Torah starts with the letter *beit*, which has the numerical value of two. This teaches us that our world is one of dualism. It links the material with the spiritual. When we join the different links together, we bring about a unity that is beyond the natural duality of this world. It was impossible for people of flesh and blood to join the *Mishkan* together. As Rashi explains, "They brought the *Mishkan* unto Moshe" (*Shemot* 39:33), for they were unable to erect it. Moshe said to the Holy One, blessed be He, "How is its erection possible by human beings?" G-d answered him, "You be busy with your hands!" Although Moshe appeared to be erecting it, in fact it set itself on end and rose of its own accord. That is why Scripture states, "…the *Mishkan* was erected" (*Shemot* 40:17), implying – by itself. The *Mishkan*, signifying unity, could only be erected through Divine intervention. Moshe merited becoming the vehicle for Divine assistance because he was the unifier of the Jewish people. Women also have the ability to reach beyond discords and join together in spite of differences. When we use this ability to unify, Hashem assists our endeavor and allows the Feminine Indwelling Presence (*Shechinah*) to rest within the Jewish people.

The Book of Vayikra – He Called (Leviticus)

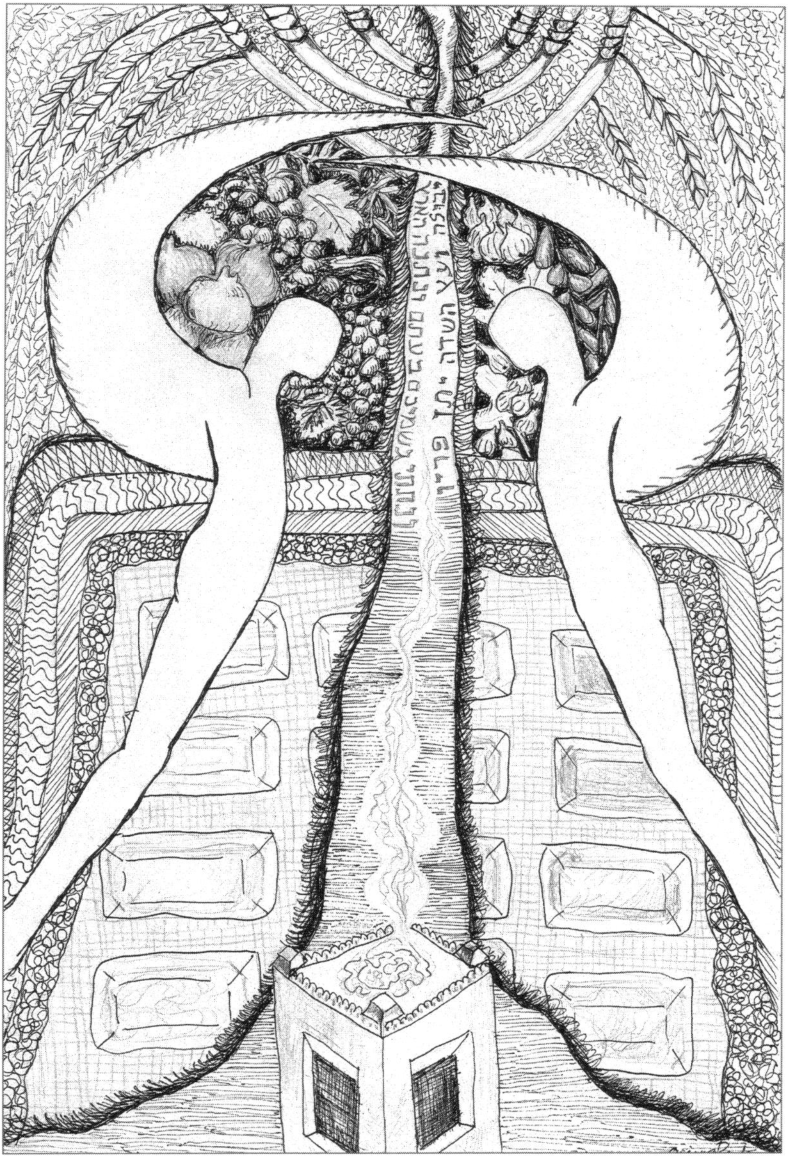

Parashat Vayikra

"When a prince has sinned…he shall bring his offering, a kid of the goats, a male without blemish" (*Vayikra* 4:22–23). The atonement for a prince who sinned unintentionally is to bring a male goat. When, however, one of the common people sins unintentionally, his atonement is a female goat. "If a soul of the common people sin in error…he shall bring his offering, a kid of the goats, a female without blemish…" (*Vayikra* 4:27–28). Why is the atonement for the prince a male goat, whereas the common people bring a female goat for the same misdemeanor?

Is Female Less Worthy Than Male?

Ibn Ezra answers that the common people bring a female goat because they are on a lower level than the prince. I have a hard time accepting this kind of statement. Why should the male represent a higher level than the female? Does this imply that men are more important than women? The modern Torah commentators emphasize that this is not the case at all. The reason why women are exempt from certain *mitzvot* is that they are naturally in tune with the will of G-d, and therefore, do not need as many *mitzvot* to keep them on track. However, some of us sense deep down that these kinds of explanations are apologetic rationalizations designed to smooth over the many statements in the Torah that seem to denigrate women. It is hard to cover up the fact that the Jewish man thanks G-d every morning for not having been created a woman. Women cannot count as legitimate witnesses in a Jewish court (*Shavuot* 30a), and a woman cannot become a rabbi according to the Torah tradition. Many of the more classic commentaries explain that women are exempt from certain *mitzvot* so as to be able to serve their husbands. The standard teacher in a woman's Torah seminary will gracefully skip this sort of commentary.

External Social Ranks

Western culture emphasizes competition and striving towards becoming "Number One." People compare and measure themselves against one another. The higher they score on the scale of wealth, beauty, and youthfulness, the more valuable and important they consider themselves. On the surface, it might seem that the Torah also evaluates people according to a system of ranks. The highest level is that of the *Kohen*, followed by the Levite, and finally the Israelite. Lower down on the list is the Jewish woman, just slightly above the Jewish slave who is followed by the gentile. Yet, it is only the competitive western outlook that makes us view the Jewish system of ranks as reflecting the intrinsic worth of any person. Although the *Kohen* is allotted certain honors, it does not imply that the *Kohen* is a better person than the common Jew. Neither is a prince necessarily spiritually superior to a commoner. The Midrash states, "I call heaven and earth to witness, be it Jew or non-Jew, man or woman, manservant or maidservant – only according to their actions will the spirit of holiness rest upon them" (*Yalkut Shimoni*, *Shoftim* 4:42).

No Value Judgment

Returning to the subject of the sacrifice of goats, it is possible to understand the Torah law in a way that does not place any value judgment on the male versus the female goat. Rather, the law contains compassion for the poor man while making the ritual meaningful for the rich. When raising goats it is practical to keep one male goat for about twenty female goats, since it can breed with several females. Therefore, a poor family with only twenty goats cannot give up their one male goat, for to do so would be to put the family out of business. The rich man has many males and females and the loss of one male will not devastate his family. The goats of both genders each have their place of importance and the farmer thanks the Creator every day for providing the indispensable male and female goats to sustain his family.

Not a Question of Importance

We are all designated to accomplish a particular mission in this world, and the way we perform our task determines our greatness, rather than where we rank in the apparent hierarchy of Judaism. The purpose of these external ranks is only to ensure that society runs smoothly, without having any relation to the value of a person. We all ultimately have to subordinate ourselves to the will of G-d. Therefore, why should it matter where we are on the social ladder? When our goal becomes serving Hashem to the best of our ability, the question of who is more important becomes irrelevant. Clearly, this does not justify someone using his position to take advantage of those beneath him, just like it is unacceptable when a leader turns into a dictator.

Equal Before G-d

When comparing the sacrifice of the prince to that of the common people, Rabbi S.R. Hirsch explains that the difference in the social status of the prince and the commoner affects neither their moral distinction, nor their ability to get closer to G-d. The purpose of all sacrifices is to be pleasing to G-d, and each person bringing a sacrifice should strive to perform the will of G-d on earth. Both the goat of the prince and that of the commoner undergo the same procedure of sacrifice according to the precepts of the Torah. These sin offerings equally become subordinated to the sharp knife of the ritual slaughter, according to the command of G-d. When the least "important person" preserves his moral integrity, his sacrifice will join the same altar as that of the prince. They are equal in value, as is every mitzvah when performed for the sake of G-d. Keeping this perspective in mind makes it easier to detach ourselves from the competitive attitude of western culture, and liberates us from comparing ourselves with men.

Parashat Tzav

This week's *parashah* begins by describing the burnt offering, while the end of the previous *parashah* described the guilt offering which a person must bring to atone for having denied that he stole. The most important condition upon which all the sacrifices depend, is hinted at in the juxtaposition between *Parashat Vayikra* and *Parashat Tzav*.

With Clean Hands

The end of *Parashat Vayikra* proclaims, "It shall be, because he has sinned, and incurred guilt, that he shall restore that which he took violently away..." (*Vayikra* 5:23). *Parashat Tzav* begins, "...and this is the law of the burnt offering" (*Vayikra* 6:2). The connection between the two sections teaches us that if you desire to bring an offering, do not steal anything from anyone. "For I, Hashem love justice. I hate robbery with burnt offerings" (*Yesha'yahu* 61:8). "When will I accept the burnt offering which you bring? When you have cleaned your hands from robbery, as King David states, 'Who shall ascend unto the mountain of G-d and who shall stand in his holy place? [He that has] clean hands and a pure heart'" (*Midrash Tanchuma, Tzav* 1 quoting *Tehillim* 24:3–4). This teaches us that honesty in monetary matters is an absolute condition for offering any sacrifice in the sanctuary. Our worship of G-d for all generations is defined by this lesson, even when we do not have a sanctuary. There can be neither sacrifice nor any kind of closeness to G-d, except when the deeds of our mundane life are purified from the smallest tinge of harming our neighbor. We cannot separate the two. Offering a sacrifice without adhering to upright and honest behavior is the kind of rite against which the prophets of Israel fought an eternal battle.

Like the First Man

This principle is also hinted at in the beginning of the book of *Vayikra*, at the onset of the entire teaching about the sacrifices. "If any person of you offers an offering unto Hashem…" (*Vayikra* 1:2). The Hebrew word used to describe "any person" is *adam*. This is an exception from the usual usage of the word *ish*. Rashi, therefore asks, "Why is this term for "a person" employed here? Since *adam* also means the first man, its use suggests the following comparison: Just as the first man did not sacrifice anything acquired dishonestly, since everything in the world belonged to him, so you too, shall not offer anything acquired dishonestly" (*Vayikra Rabbah* 2:7). The connection between honest behavior and the offerings of G-d is only hinted at rather than written directly in the Torah, as it is supposed to be understood intuitively. This important principle is so basic to the Torah that it is not necessary to speak about it straightforwardly.

The Extent of Robbery

"If a soul sins, and commits a trespass against Hashem, and denies unto his neighbor, a charge, or a deposit, or a thing taken away by violence, or has wronged his neighbor…because he has sinned, and incurred guilt, he shall restore that which he took…and he shall bring the guilt offering unto Hashem, a ram without blemish…" (*Vayikra* 5:21–25). These verses enumerate several possible ways of damaging the property of one's fellow, and allude to what extent the concept of stealing pertains. Not only bank robbery and pick pocketing but any kind of deviation from proper business practices in the market of life is considered stealing. Even finding a lost object, and swearing that he didn't find it, obligates the person to bring a sacrifice. The Talmud asks, "What is called robbery?" Rabbi Chisda answers, "Someone who says, 'Go and return, go and return' this is robbery" (*Baba Metzia* 111a).

Thus, pushing off a person to whom one owes money, by telling him to come back later, is considered stealing, because it costs him his time.

Stealing from Our Children

The interdependence between proper interpersonal relationships and closeness to G-d pertains directly to the role of the Jewish mother. I once knew a very "spiritual" woman who loved to pray. Every Friday night, following candle lighting, she would leave her five small children in her candle lit dining room, as she ran off to the synagogue to encounter G-d. How often does it happen that we are involved in "important" *mitzvot* at the expense of our children? There is a famous story about how the entire congregation was waiting impatiently for Rabbi Yisrael Salanter to lead them in the holy prayer of *Kol Nidrei* on the evening of Yom Kippur. After a delay of more than an hour, he finally arrived. The reason for his delay was a crying infant that he happened to hear on his way to the synagogue. While the mother had left her youngster alone in order to pray, Rabbi Yisrael Salanter understood that comforting this frightened child took precedence over leading the entire congregation in the Yom Kippur service.

Especially prior to *Pesach*, when we are commanded to sacrifice a sheep together with the family or close neighbors (*Shemot* 12:3–4), we are reminded that our freedom to serve Hashem is interdependent with our ability to establish healthy relationships with the people in our lives, particularly with our children. Remember that dust is not *chametz*, and our children are not a *Pesach* sacrifice.

Parashat Shemini

A central theme in *Parashat Shemini* is immersing in the *mikvah* (ritual bath), which is one of the three primary *mitzvot* designated for the Jewish woman, in addition to the *challah* offering and lighting the Shabbat candles. Immersing in a *mikvah* has the power to change the status of either a person or a vessel by spiritually purifying it.

Returning to Eden

Rabbi Aryeh Kaplan explains in *Waters of Eden* that the purpose of the *mikvah* is to bring us back to the Garden of Eden, from where we were expelled when partaking from the Tree of Knowledge. Immersing in the *mikvah* enables us to rise from the fallen state caused by eating from the Tree of Knowledge and to reconnect us with the perfected state of Eden. An allusion to this is found in the word *mikvah*, consisting of the Hebrew letters *mem, kuf, vav, heh*, which has the same Hebrew letters as the word *koma* spelled *kuf, vav, mem, heh*, meaning rising or standing tall. Since human mortality is also a consequence of our fallen state, returning to the Garden of Eden requires purification from everything associated with death by immersing in the *mikvah*. Coming to the Holy Temple and entering the sacredness of marital intimacy are ways to re-enter the Garden of Eden in a spiritual sense. Menstruation is related to death as it implies the loss of potential life. Therefore, the Torah requires the Jewish married woman to purify herself spiritually after her monthly period. By immersing in the waters of the *mikvah*, she prepares herself for marital relations – her personal return to Eden.

The Mikvah Represents the Womb

Rabbi Aryeh Kaplan explains that the *mikvah* represents the womb. When a woman enters the *mikvah*, it is as though she returns to the womb, and when she emerges, she is born anew. Converts undergo a similar process. They must immerse in a *mikvah* to become reborn as Jews. Since the womb represents the quintessence of womanhood, the Jewish woman embodies spiritual renewal through her immersion in the *mikvah* following her menstrual cycle, which marks both the end and beginning of a new reproductive cycle of conceiving potential life.

The process of motherhood trains the woman to overcome her ego, the essence of inflexibility. It was this ego that made the first woman susceptible to the seduction of the serpent tempting, "...and you shall be as gods..." (*Bereishit* 3:5). The desire to "be as gods" is expressed as a compulsion for the stability of being in control. Raising children gives us the ability to retain our flexibility and willingness to undergo personal change and renewal. This is parallel to immersion in the *mikvah*, which expresses willingness to focus on something greater than ourselves, and thus enables us to emerge reborn. In this way, we connect with the Source of life that allows us to return to Eden in a spiritual sense.

Relationship Like Water

The word *mikvah* is associated with water as in "a gathering of water" (*Vayikra* 11:36). Water is fluid and embodies the essence of impermanence and flexibility. It will move to leave room for any object placed in its midst. This is similar to the woman who, on a physical level, every month creates the beginning of a new being. This potential life is either expelled through her monthly cycle, or implanted in her womb, which she expands to encompass the needs of her unborn child. On an emotional level, as mothers, our little ones constantly teach us to adapt and remain flexible.

For a relationship to work, we need the flexibility of water embracing whoever immerses in it. When we are too fixated on the way we expect things to be done, we get into confrontations. Letting go of expectations allows us to adapt to the needs of others and merge with them. Womanhood teach us to become naturally inclined towards flexibility. Pregnancy, childbirth and childrearing all contribute to our ability to make room for another human being. Perhaps this is why women associate with the waters of the *mikvah*. We have been blessed with the ability to bring the experiences of our life cycle into our relationships and teach ourselves, our spouses, and children to overcome egocentric attitudes and behavior.

If I want to get any work done while I care for my baby, I need to move quickly from task to task, so I can keep him interested and amused. I hang the laundry outside where the birds sing and the grass grows. Then I swish the water on the soapy dishes. After picking fresh vegetables and watering the garden, I return to the kitchen sink scrubbing colorful vegetables. To keep my child happy, I need to let go of the satisfaction of getting a job completely finished by a certain time. I have to be spontaneous and "go with the flow."

Merging Manmade With Divine

"Nevertheless a fountain or pit, where in there is a gathering of water, shall be clean..." (*Vayikra* 11:36). From this verse the laws of the *mikvah* are derived. The word *ma'ayan*, which means fountain or spring, teaches that the water of the *mikvah* must be natural. From the next word, *bor* meaning pit or cistern, we learn that the receptacle for the *mikvah* can be manmade. The word *mikvah* itself means gathering. Thus, the *mikvah* gathers and connects the natural water created by Hashem with the manmade. It is also a woman's task to connect the manmade with the Divine. While carrying life within her, she becomes G-d's partner in creation. By taking good care of herself during pregnancy, she nurtures the baby that G-d granted her. Similarly, she becomes a partner with G-d in the creation of her home. Besides furnishing and decorating it, through the mitzvah of Shabbat candles, she allows Divinity to permeate her home. Her mitzvah of taking *challah* elevates the Divine sparks contained in the food, which she cooks. By immersing in the *mikvah*, she brings G-d into her relationships, and thereby sanctifies her family life.

Parashat Tazria

The previous *parashah* concluded with the mitzvah that the children of Israel sanctify themselves: "For I am Hashem your G-d; you shall therefore sanctify yourselves, for I am holy…" (*Vayikra* 11:44). *Parashat Tazria* opens with the laws of purification after birth: "If a woman has conceived seed, and given birth to a male…" (*Vayikra* 12:2).

Holy Union

Ba'al HaTurim explains that the Torah juxtaposes the description of the woman who has conceived with the command to be holy in order to teach that one must sanctify oneself at the time of intimate relations. In Judaism, marital relations can be one of the holiest acts a person ever performs. Through marital relations, one becomes a partner in creation. Even when no physical children are conceived, the holy union between husband and wife causes souls to be brought down from Heaven. These souls later enter the bodies of converts as the Midrash explains when referring to, "the souls that they [Avraham and Sarah] had made in Charan" (*Bereishit Rabbah* 84:4 quoting *Bereishit* 12:5).

The Fruit of Their Affection

Why is the verse describing the woman who conceives juxtaposed with the section about prohibited foods? Ramban explains in *Igeret Ha-Kodesh* that eating forbidden foods can influence the embryo negatively and cause the baby to be born without spiritual sensitivity. Just like food is a factor, imagination and thought also influence the embryo. When husband and wife unite with thoughts of love, the *Shechinah* rests between them, and their child becomes the fruit of their pure desires and affection. This principle can be understood in light of our current medical knowledge. A pregnant woman is instructed to avoid x-rays, especially during the first trimester of pregnancy. The reason given is that while the fetus is forming its initial features it is most susceptible to outside influence. From this we can infer that at the time of conception the embryo is even more impressionable, and thus greatly influenced by the mental state of the parents.

The Image of Love

"Rabbi Yitzchak said in the name of Rabbi Ami, when a woman reaches climax first, she gives birth to a son. When a man gives seed first, she gives birth to a daughter, as it states: 'If a woman has conceived seed, and given birth to a male...'" (*Niddah* 31a, quoting Vayikra 12:2). It is difficult to understand how the sex of the child conceived depends on whether the man or the woman came first during the act of intercourse. *Sha'arei Aharon* explains that a male child is conceived when the woman reaches climax first because of her passion for her husband. All her thoughts center on her husband, and she visualizes his appearance and character in her heart. The power of this visualization causes her to give birth to a male similar to her husband. In the same way, Ya'acov *Avinu* (our father) carved patterns on the sticks that he placed before the flock while they were mating. As a result, they gave birth to offspring speckled and spotted like the patterns on the sticks (*Bereishit* 30:37–38). If animals are able to influence their offspring by means of mental visualization, how much more so can we expect this of human beings, whose mind is so much more developed?

Transmitting Divine Light

Ramban, in *Igeret HaKodesh*, emphasizes how G-d gave man the ability to create with the power of his thought. An example of this is found in the Talmud, "Rabbi Yochanan was accustomed to sit at the gates of the *mikvah*. He said, 'When the daughters of Israel come up from bathing, they look at me and have children as handsome as I'" (*Berachot* 20a). Ramban explains that when the image of the holy Rabbi Yochanan was imprinted in the woman's mind upon returning from her immersion prior to uniting with her husband, her thoughts would shape and beautify her child. This notion prompts the following questions, why would Rabbi Yochanan care that women give birth to children as handsome as he? Moreover, how could it be permissible for a woman to think of Rabbi Yochanan while having relations with her husband? Understanding the secret of the power of thought will help us shed light on these questions. The masters of Kabbalah explain that a person's thoughts derive from the highest part of his soul, drawn from the upper spheres. Thought has the power to rise up and draw down supernal light. A person who masters this ability glows from rays of Divine light. In this way, the early *Chassidim* would cause the Divine Presence to dwell below. Holy thoughts, therefore, have the power to increase and bless things on earth. This is the secret of the oil cruise of the prophet Elisha and the jug of flour, which remained full (2 *Melachim*, Chapter 4). Rabbi Yochanan's beauty was not just physical; it was the manifestation of the Divine light he brought down by causing his thoughts to cleave to the heavenly regions. Therefore, when a woman would look at his face, she was not just gazing at another man, but at the Divine presence, which he reflected. This vision would connect her so deeply to G-d that she could transmit Rabbi Yochanan's holiness to the children she conceived.

Education Starts With Conception

Modern psychology has established that a woman's thoughts during pregnancy influence her fetus. For example, a woman anticipating the birth of her child with pleasure and happiness causes her baby to be born with a self-confident disposition. Our ancient Jewish tradition knew more than what modern research is just recently discovering. Not only do the feelings and thoughts of the mother during pregnancy influence her embryo; even at the time of conception her thoughts have power to shape her unborn child. "Before you were conceived in the womb, I knew you…" (*Yirmeyahu* 1:5). Since our thoughts during conception have such a great effect on the fetus, we must try to think only of holy and pure matters during intimate relations in order to draw down holy souls, for Jewish child education begins at the time of conception.

Parashat Metzora

This week's *parashah*, like the previous one, deals with spiritual purification so relevant to the time period between Pesach and Shavuot. "If a woman has a discharge of blood, where blood flows from her body, she shall be *niddah* for seven days..." (*Vayikra* 15:19).

Why Separate the Menstruating Woman?

The Torah tells us that from the time a woman has her period, until she immerses in the *mikvah*, she has the status of a *niddah*. The concept of *niddah* is related to the word *naddad*, meaning to wander, separate or remove. During this period, the woman separates herself from any physical contact with her husband. What is the underlying reason for *niddah*? Why does a woman have to separate from her husband every month? The laws of *niddah* and menstruation are difficult to understand. They are *chukim* (statutes) whose ultimate reasons are beyond human comprehension. Nevertheless, we may attempt to explore and uncover some of the reasons concerning the concept of *niddah*.

Unlike the Taboos of Primitive Cultures

People may think that the Torah laws regarding the menstruating woman are similar to the taboos of many primitive cultures that attribute to her some "evil force." It is therefore important to highlight that according to Jewish law, ritual impurity is not exclusively connected with the menstruating woman. Earlier, in *Parashat Metzora*, the Torah mentioned the laws dealing with the purification of a man who has a discharge. He needs to purify himself in a spring of water, since the *mikvah* does not qualify to purify such strong impurity. Furthermore, upon purification, he must bring a sin offering, as recognition for being healed from a sickness (*Vayikra* 15:1–15). Rambam points out that this is not the case regarding the menstruating woman since her period is a natural occurrence, and not a sickness. The definition of ritual impurity in the Torah is contact with death. The menstrual period is included in this category since it, in fact, is the expulsion of potential life. For the same reason the male semen causes ritual impurity as well (see Rashi, *Shemot* 19:15).

A Result of Eating from the Tree of Knowledge

The impurity of death is a result of the sin of Adam and Chava. We were supposed to have lived eternal life in the Garden of Eden. However, the sin of eating from the Tree of Knowledge brought imperfection and death into the world. When Chava was told, "…I will greatly increase the pain of your childbearing…" (*Bereishit* 3:16), the words "I will greatly increase" referred to the pain of menstruation (*Iruvin* 100b), which is part of the reproductive cycle. The expulsion of mankind from the Garden obstructed the natural harmony between man and woman. However, G-d gave us ways to return to Eden. Both entering the holy Temple and intimate relations between husband and wife are pathways of returning to the Garden. Marital relations are compared to the sanctuary, which is like a miniature Garden of Eden. When a person was in an impure (*tumah*) state, he was absolutely forbidden to enter the holy Temple under the severest of penalties. The fact that this impurity is not physical, but primarily involves the soul is learned from the verse "…you shall not make your **souls** unclean…" (*Vayikra* 11:44). Thus, before entering the Temple, or having marital relations, one must be spiritually purified by immersion in a *mikvah*. The power of the *mikvah* to return us to the state of Eden is alluded to in the story of Adam and Chava in the Garden of Eden. Rabbi Aryeh Kaplan notes in *Waters of Eden* that the story is suddenly interrupted by the description of the river, which went out of Eden. The reason for this interruption is to provide a way to return to Eden even before being expelled, according to the principle that Hashem makes the healing precede the wound (*Megillah* 13b). The natural rainwater collected in the *mikvah* connects us with the river, which brings us back to the Garden of Eden.

A Cleansing Process

On a pragmatic level, the laws of *niddah* have a beneficial effect on marriage. Physical separation compels husband and wife to relate on a mental and spiritual level, and prevents them from merely smoothing out conflicts with a kiss. Actually, the monthly separation between husband and wife helps restore and intensify their original love. Each time the wife returns fresh from the *mikvah*, their relationship is renewed as if they had just experienced another honeymoon. Rabbeinu Bachaya writes that since menstruation is the consequence of eating from the Tree of Knowledge, the capacity of purification through the menstrual flow is a distinct human feature. Although uncomfortable, the menstrual period is actually beneficial for the future fetus. Menstruation cleanses the woman and expels any unnecessary substances accumulated during the month, together with the uterine lining. This way the fetus is formed by the purest and highest quality blood, preparing it to receive the Divine influence, the light of the soul. This can be compared to steel which is polished from rust in order to reflect the sunlight. It is interesting that a woman bleeds after birth for approximately the same amount of time as the duration of the collective nine menstrual periods, which she has missed. All this teaches us that in Judaism the menstruating woman is far from being considered someone sick and shameful. On the contrary, she is regarded as being in the process of cleansing in order to enter the holy sanctuary of marital relations – the gateway to Eden.

Parashat Acharei Mot

This week's *parashah*, which lists all the forbidden sexual relationships, is also read on Yom Kippur. It includes the prohibition to marry a woman and her sister: "Neither shall you take a wife to her sister, to make her a rival, and uncover her nakedness, beside the other during her life time" (*Vayikra* 18:18). Rashi learns from the phrase, "during her life time" that if he divorces his wife, he is not allowed to marry her sister as long as his first wife is still alive. Rabbi S.R. Hirsch notes that marrying the wife's sister is the only sexual prohibition, which is nullified after death, and moreover, the only prohibition about which Scripture states the reason, to avoid "making her a rival" (*litzror*).

Concern for the Feelings of Sisters

According to Ramban, no reason was necessary to give for the prohibition of marrying a mother and daughter, since the daughter comes from the body of the mother, and the Torah therefore forbids marrying both even after one of them dies. Most of the sexual prohibitions mentioned in our *parashah* can never be permitted for they intrinsically contradict the order of creation as Rambam explains: "Marital relations between the root and the branch, between a man and his mother, or his daughter are abominations...therefore, it is prohibited to marry a woman and her mother, the wife of the father or of the son" (*The Guide to the Perplexed*, Part 3, Chapter 49). However, marrying two sisters is not included in the abomination of cohabiting with the root and the branch, since both are on the level of branch. Why then does the Torah forbid a man to marry two sisters? The reason is out of concern for the sisters' feelings. This only applies as long as both sisters are alive.

Sisterly Love

Rashi notes that the word *litzror* in our verse is connected with the word *tzarah* – a rival. Although a man in Biblical times was permitted to marry more than one wife, Ramban explains that it is not considerate to marry two sisters and thereby cause them to become rivals, since sisters are supposed to love one another. As *Sefer HaChinuch* explains, "…my heart tells me in this matter that Scripture forbade marrying two sisters, since the Master of peace desires peace among all His creatures, and especially between those whose nature is to be at peace. There should not be strife and competition between them all day long" (*Sefer HaChinuch,* Mitzvah 206). Similarly HaRivash writes that two sisters who are beloved to one another should not be set up against each other to cause jealousy and conflict between them. Even after a man divorces one sister, he is forbidden to marry the other, out of consideration that the other sister may become jealous when she comes by to visit. However, after death, discord and jealousy have passed. Then it is actually a mitzvah to marry the sister of the deceased wife, in order that she may take upon herself raising her sister's children.

Sisters Need Space

Rabbi Ya'acov Tzvi Mecklenburg explains that *litzror* means to link. When a man marries two wives, he ties them together and makes them like one body through their effort to run the household. Just like items tied together cannot be separated without untying the knot that binds them, so are the wives unable to separate one from the other without separating from their husband to whom they are linked by marriage. Tying both of them together by marriage is called *litzror.* The wives being attached to the other without being able to separate is called *tzarot* – "rivals." Rabbi S.R. Hirsch adds that when people are tied together too tightly, it causes constriction and hatred. Therefore, the same word means both "linked" and "rival." The Torah teaches that a man may not marry two sisters, causing them to become rivals by tying them together in one marriage. Because of the natural closeness of sisters, the Torah is concerned that each sister has her own personal space to develop herself and to receive the opportunity to express her own individuality.

I remember how much it used to bother me as a child when my younger sister would imitate me. I felt my personal identity was suffocating, and I had to struggle to be free to choose my own style of clothes, colors and interests. It was very important for me to have my own friends and I couldn't stand it when my sister always tagged along. If two sisters would be married to the same husband they would never have their own individual space. There is another important reason why sisters need to live their own separate lives. Sisters are supposed to be each other's best friends. Our friends are able to guide us because they are not blinded by our emotional tendencies. They do not share the same experience, and therefore see the situation from a different perspective. If our sister were to be part of our own daily family situation, how could she retain a separate perspective as a friend? If she would be part of our own household, whom would we confide in about the intimate challenges within our family? The Torah is concerned that we keep our sister as a disinterested ally to rely on. Who else would understand and care as much?

Sisters Are Like a Double Edged Sword

Although it is the nature of sisters to love one another, they simultaneously have inherent tendencies towards competition and jealousy. The reason for this might be that we only become jealous of someone we identify with, someone to whom we feel similar and equal. It is therefore, not the nature of a woman to be jealous of her mother or daughter. Yet, stemming from the same branch, the closeness of sisters can either cause burning jealousy, or be the root of the greatest love and friendship. The Divine commandment not to marry two sisters during their lifetime shows sensitivity to the nature of sisterhood, and highlights how important love between sisters is to G-d. Therefore, it is our human responsibility to assure that the natural peace and love among sisters does not turn into jealousy, hatred and strife. Friends may come and go on the paths of our lives, yet our sister is always there in times of need. We must cherish and nourish this sisterly bond in every way, and work on ourselves to be a kind and reliable sister. Our different styles or levels of religiosity should never be allowed to interfere with the natural love of sisterhood.

Parashat Kedoshim

Parashat Kedoshim describes the special laws that preserve the holiness of the Jewish people, through which they distinguish themselves from the rest of the nations. "Do not prostitute your daughter, to cause her to be a harlot, lest the land fall to harlotry, and the land become full of lust" (*Vayikra* 19:29). This verse refers to a person who hands his unmarried daughter over to have intimate relations not for the sake of marriage (Rashi, based on *Sanhedrin* 76a). Rabbi S.R. Hirsch adds that this prohibition applies to every premarital and extramarital intercourse. Similarly, Rabbi Aryeh Kaplan explains in *Waters of Eden* that according to the Torah's definition, harlotry includes all forms of premarital sex, and has nothing to do with payment for the act.

Holiness is Keeping Apart

The prohibition against premarital sex undoubtedly differs from what is accepted in modern secular circles. Even certain singles who consider themselves religious may be tempted to succumb to the western standards of acceptable social behavior in this respect. People might defend themselves saying, "We are no longer youngsters, and we need to have a life." Wanting to enjoy the pleasures of life, they rationalize that they must "try out" their partner before being ready to commit themselves to marriage. This attitude stands in sharp contrast with the holiness that G-d expects of His Chosen People. Actually holiness itself is related to separateness. The first time the word "holy" is used is when G-d set aside the Shabbat from the six days of creation and sanctified it (*Bereishit* 2:3). Therefore, living a holy life implies being able to keep apart in spite of the appeal which the loose life entails.

Marriage Depends on Spiritual Compatibility

Marriage in Hebrew is called *kedushin* which literally means holiness. Marriage is a holy institution because it is first and foremost a sacred union, based upon spiritual and emotional affinity followed by physical congeniality (not vice versa). The belief that it is necessary to test sexual compatibility before committing oneself to the other in marriage assumes that the physical aspect is the primary component of marriage and that the other components will come about in its wake. When people get married mainly for the sake of pleasure, it is no wonder that divorce is so common. As soon as the initial attraction wears off, there is little left to bind the marriage partners together.

Love Comes After Marriage

If we believe that the soul is our essence and the body is only its vessel, it follows that all we need to check out before marriage is spiritual compatibility. When a wife was selected for Yitzchak, the emphasis was on virtuous character. As *Kli Yakar* explains regarding Rivkah, when a person possesses the character trait of *chesed* (loving/kindness), then all the other good qualities are easily attained. In the same manner, when there is closeness of spirit between two people, then physical compatibility can be achieved. It is interesting to note that the verse describing the marriage of Yitzchak and Rivkah reads, "…she became his wife; and he loved her…" (*Bereishit* 24:67). This clearly indicates that love comes after marriage. Love is the result of two people dedicating their lives to the building of a spiritual union. This is congruent with Scott Peck's definition of love in his book *The Road Less Traveled*. He writes that love is to extend oneself for the sake of the spiritual growth of someone other than oneself. Conversely, indulging in premarital sex is based on the assumption that love is characterized by receiving physical pleasure. Since this kind of love is essentially selfish, based on taking rather than giving, it is unlikely to endure.

The Innate Holiness of the Jewish Daughter

Regarding our verse prohibiting the father from profaning the holiness of his daughter, Rabbi S.R. Hirsch points out that the term "do not profane" assumes that the daughters of Israel possess an innate holiness, which is subject to profanation. "The Torah presumes an inborn greater degree of chaste modesty and morality in women. In general it is not from women but from the degeneration of the male sex that morality sinks. If the Law succeeds to save the morality of the men, the moral nature of the women will by itself keep it within the limits of decency." Most women seek the kind of relationship that focuses on the spiritual rather than the physical. We yearn for stability and permanence in order to build a nurturing and lasting attachment. It is our responsibility not to allow any corrupt influence in society or extraneous pressure to pervert the innate modesty and holiness of the Jewish woman.

Parashat Emor

This week's *parashah* tells the story of the son born from a Jewish mother and an Egyptian father who blasphemed Hashem. His mother, Shlomit bat Dibri, was an extremely attractive woman. One day an Egyptian taskmaster in charge of one hundred and twenty Jewish slaves, noticed her, when he went on his usual rounds to the homes of his workers in order to assemble them. With his eye on Shlomit, he called her husband out to work and returned to her house pretending to be her husband. When Shlomit's husband saw the Egyptian man exit his house, he was concerned and asked his wife whether he had touched her. She answered, "Yes, but I thought that he was you." Once the taskmaster found out that Shlomit's husband was aware of what had taken place, he whipped him. This was the Egyptian man that Moshe later killed when he saw with *Ruach HaKodesh* that he deserved death for committing adultery (*Midrash Tanchuma, Shemot* 9).

Intermarriage – The Exception in Israel

The son of the Israelite woman, whose father was an Egyptian man, went out among the children of Israel, and this son of the Israelite woman and a man of Israel strove together in the camp; the Israelite woman's son blasphemed the name of Hashem, and cursed. They brought him to Moshe, and his mother's name was Shlomit, the daughter of Dibri, of the tribe of Dan (*Vayikra* 24:10–11).

It seems peculiar that the name of the person who cursed is not mentioned at all, whereas only the name of his mother is stated. Rashi explains that Scripture publicly mentions her name to tell the praise of Israel, that among all the Jewish women during the entire Egyptian exile, she alone had relations with an Egyptian. *Be'er Yitzchak* clarifies how we learn Israel's praise from Shlomit's deviation. When someone acts in a strange and unexpected way, people want to know who acted this way, whether for good or for bad. The fact that the name of this Israelite woman is noted clearly shows that although her fellow Jews had lived in the perverse Egyptian society for years, being the victim of a relation with a non-Jewish man was considered foreign and strange to them. Shlomit bat Dibri stood out among them, and therefore they noticed her name.

The Power of Speech by Way of Example

Although one should never automatically blame the victim, in this particular case, Rashi explains that Scripture hints through the meaning of her name that Shlomit was disposed towards being assaulted. The name Shlomit is related to the Hebrew salutation "Shalom," and *Dibri* means talkative. She was called Shlomit bat Dibri because she was always babbling: "How are you?", "how are you?", and "how are you?" She was a *bat Dibri*; talking with any man in the street, and this is what eventually caused her to get into trouble (Rashi, *Vayikra* 24:11). Scripture refers to the uncontrolled speech of the mother of the blasphemer to teach us that a mother has a special responsibility to teach her children proper behavior by example. The way we use our Divine capability of speech has repercussions in our children. This does not imply that the mother is responsible for her children's actions. It certainly is not for us to judge why many righteous parents have children who deviate from the path. We are also not in a position to judge the children, who may be righteous in disguise. Every person has free choice. However, within the intricate makeup of a person's personality; there is an important aspect of character that reflects the nature of the mother to whom he or she was attached throughout the formative years.

Transmitting Her Essence to Her Children

We would have expected the verse to simply read, "The son of the Israelite woman whose name was Shlomit bat Dibri went out." Why did Scripture mention the name of Shlomit only after the cursing of her son? Rabbi S.R. Hirsch explains that it was only through her son's cursing that his mother's ethical flaw became revealed. A possible explanation for the stronger affinity between a child and his mother than his father is that a fetus is created from the blood of his mother, and grows within her for nine months. Even after birth, the infant is nourished directly by her. For this reason, the kings of Israel are often mentioned in Scripture by the name of their mother. When a person is righteous, modest and virtuous, it is often a result of his mother's positive influence. The good branch testifies to the virtue of the root. Therefore, King David said about himself, "…I am your servant the son of your handmaid…" (*Tehillim* 116:16). Likewise Radak comments that King David mentioned his mother because she was primary in his formation.

Children Learn from Deeds Rather Than Creeds

Today, a mother might be confused by the many different approaches to educating her children. Should she apply a strict disciplinarian method of education or opt for more permissive modern approaches of childrearing? There is no one correct technique of education that can be applied equally to all children. "Educate the youth according to **his** way…" (*Mishlei* 22:6). Many children turn out to be virtuous human beings regardless of the technique applied in raising them. As an old friend whispered into my ear, "If you love Torah and what matters to you is becoming close to G-d, this is what your child picks up, no matter which educational approach you follow." Her words convey a deep lesson about child education. It is the same lesson that we inversely learn from Shlomit bat Dibri. Her son turned out the way he did, not so much as a result of how he was raised, but rather because of where his mother was holding personally. Her misuse of the faculty of speech was a seed implanted within her son, taken to its extreme when he blasphemed G-d with this same power of speech.

Yet, the Torah does not want us to feel guilty in case our children, G-d forbid, don't turn out exactly as we may have hoped. Certainly, it would be against the Torah to point a finger at others and blame the mother for the behavior of her children. As mothers, we must realize our great responsibility in building the character of our children. They are influenced by who we are rather than by what we preach. On the other hand, we must keep in mind that we can only do our best. Many unknown factors shape the final outcome of our children. May our continued endeavor to perfect our character and get closer to G-d eventually rub off on our children!

Parashat Behar

This week's *parashah* describes the special relationship between the Jewish people, the Land of Israel and the laws of the land through which we actualize this relationship. "Hashem spoke to Moshe in Mount Sinai, saying, speak to the children of Israel, and say to them, when you come to the land which I give you, then the land shall keep Shabbat to Hashem" (*Vayikra* 25:1–2).

To Earn Her Love

Why does it state "The land which I give you" in present tense? Had G-d not already promised the children of Israel the gift of the land repeatedly? The present tense alludes to the fact that we can never take our ownership of the Land of Israel for granted. Whereas other countries belong to the nations because they were born there, the children of Israel constantly have to earn the right to their land. The land can be compared to a bride whose love must be won by the worthy suitor, as she will only yield her fruits to a deserving groom. This is different from the relationship of the other nations to their land, which they call "fatherland." Just like a child can expect the love of his parents without having to deserve it by his deeds, so is the relationship between the nations and their land automatic and often taken for granted. No special love and dedication is needed to prove the right to their land.

Tending the Garden of Marriage

A man comes from his parents but leaves them in order to unite with his wife, as it states: "That is why a man leaves his father and his mother, and cleaves to his wife" (*Bereishit* 2:24). Likewise, Avraham was told, "Go from your country, from your birthplace, and from the house of your father, to the land..." (*Bereishit* 12:1). He had to leave his native country and go towards the land, which G-d would show him just like a man must leave his parents in order to live with his wife. I believe that one of the reasons why it is so hard to stay married in our time, is because we don't realize the difference between the relationship of children to their parents and husbands to their wives. While dating, the young suitor endeavors to sweep away his sweetheart with clever wit and gentlemanly demeanor. Once he has won her over, he no longer feels it necessary to prove his love for her. She resents being taken for granted, and withholds some of her efforts on his behalf. This starts the vicious circle of mutual withdrawal that has broken so many homes. The Torah teaches us what every gardener already knows. It is not enough to plant the seed and then expect the tree to grow by itself. Without constantly tending it by watering and weeding, one cannot expect that the tree will bear fruit.

Time Off for the Honor of G-d

"...Then the land shall keep Shabbat to Hashem." Through keeping the laws of *shemittah,* the children of Israel prove that they do not take their ownership of the land for granted. Every seventh year is Shabbat for the land (*shemittah*) when we relinquish our ownership of the land. Our recognition that the land belongs to Hashem is what imbues it with holiness. A marriage is likewise called *kidushin*, which means holiness. It is only by means of constantly recognizing the Divinity of the land and restraining the natural desire to work it during the Shabbat year that Israel earns the right to possess it. Likewise, in order for a marriage to succeed, we need to relate to the Divine spark within our partner and let go of the desire to display ownership and dominion. Rashi explains that the laws of *shemittah* must be kept for the honor of G-d. This implies that we let the land rest for the sake of G-d's mitzvah rather than merely in order to recharge it. Similarly, when a man and a woman get married and remain together for the sake of G-d's honor, then their holy union can endure. When we let go of the quest to work the land during *shemittah*, we can dedicate ourselves to improve our relationship with G-d through increased Torah learning, mitzvah observance, and prayer. In our marriage, as well, we need to take time off from the tedious daily responsibilities of career and running the household in order to dedicate ourselves to nurture the relationship. Working on our relationship with the Divine will also help improve our relationship to each other.

Separation for the Sake of Closeness

The laws of family purity can be compared to the laws of *shemittah* since both are related to a cycle of seven. A woman must count "seven spotless days" after the end of her period, similar to the *shemittah* year that recurs every seventh year. The Shabbat year ensures that we renew our relationship with the land in the same manner that the relationship between husband and wife is constantly renewed through the separation during the period of *niddah*. Therefore, the main prohibition during *shemittah* is the prohibition against sowing. "Distance makes the heart grow fonder." The excitement of once again being permitted to dig into the fertile soil of our field after a whole year of restraint can be compared to the closeness between the husband and wife when she returns from the *mikvah* after their period of separation.

The Lesson of Faith

Keeping the laws of *shemittah* is a lesson in *emunah*. It teaches us to rely on the blessing of G-d rather than on our own handiwork. Our welfare does not depend on material pursuits alone, but on our dedication to G-d, which we demonstrate through keeping the laws of *shemittah*. Just as we need faith in the power of the *mitzvot*, so does our marriage depend on having faith in our marriage partner. Nurturing confidence, trust, and devotion within our marriage brings Divine blessing into our relationship. Focusing on our husband's good qualities makes his seed sprout forth and take root.

Parashat Bechukotai

Parashat Bechukotai enumerates the curses, of which many befell the Jewish people during the holocaust. One of the curses is lack of essential goods, including both firewood and flour. "When I have broken the staff of your bread, ten women shall bake your bread in one oven, and they shall deliver your bread again by weight" (*Vayikra* 26:26).

A Scarcity of Essentials

Rashi explains that ten women must share one oven due to the scarcity of wood. The reason why they have to deliver the bread by weight is because the grain will rot and cause the bread to crumble and break into pieces in the oven, so that the women will have to deliberately weigh the pieces in order to divide them fairly between themselves. Rabbi S.R. Hirsch comments that each oven has enough space to satisfy the need of just one household. However, because of the scarcity of bread, ten families will have to make do with what would be enough for only one family. This insufficient amount of bread must be weighed on a scale in order to ensure that no one receives more than their share.

Struggling for Survival

The Torah paints a miserable picture of deprivation. Images of such utter destitution inevitably bring the holocaust to mind. This was a time when women would search the garbage for dirty potato peels, which they would wash and pulverize in order to make potato flour for baking *matzah*. Altruism becomes a scarcity when people are struggling for their own survival. Confronted with the prospect of starvation, the survival instinct often causes people to cut down their benevolence towards others. Everyone tries to grab as much as they can for themselves to lessen the pain of their own growling stomach.

The Test of Not Taking More Than One's Share

In her book, *Strands of Fire*, Mindy Schwartz depicts the horrors of life within a concentration camp during the holocaust. As a volunteer whose task it was to divide the food, she describes the challenge of not taking more than her share. The Nazis presented the Jewish volunteers with the assignment of sharing one loaf of bread with the rest of the captives. The volunteers were supposed to cut the loaf into equal slices of bread.

> *It was not easy to slice the coarse, hard bread. I tried to be exact and to cut slices of equal size. I wanted to hurry, so as not to cause my hungry sisters, who were waiting for their dinner, unnecessary pain. I was completely absorbed in the work. When I lifted my eye for a moment, to glance at the other volunteers, I almost fell over backwards from astonishment. They each stood at the opposite side of the bread, cutting it into slices like me, but looking quickly around them, in their hunger they snatched some of the softest pieces of bread, and swallowed them. Anger and despondency overcame me. The terrible hunger was the faithful partner of the yetzer hara (evil inclination). The oppressing emptiness of the stomach dictated the stream of thoughts. Everyone was out for herself. The test was very difficult. It would become more powerful at every moment. I would tell myself, "I will overcome it" again and again as I approached my work. "I will not take more than my share," so as not to deprive my hungry sisters of theirs. Therefore, I felt so badly about the behavior of my friends. I hoped and prayed that G-d would help me to stand by my decision and continue to give me strength to withstand the test* (Mindy Schwartz, *Strands of Fire*).

Unity Overcomes Starvation

Seen in the light of the reality that Mindy describes, there is a redeeming factor in the curse that ten women would be able to share one oven (*Vayikra* 26:26). During a famine, where each person's ration is reduced to a tenth of the regular portion, it requires tremendous strength for ten women to get together and organize communal baking. By herself, no one could afford the "extravagance" of baking even the smallest loaf. Despite the discord and contention which the agony of starvation could illicit, the Torah implies that even in times of severe famine, Jewish women are able to unify and make arrangements not only of sharing one oven, but even dividing their precious goods equally to the very last crumb. It is this unity among the women that enables them to provide their family with any bread at all. What would happen if any of the women presumed to claim, "I need more, since I have a larger family!" or "I deserve a percentage of your bread as a payment for the use of my oven etc."? These demands would most likely make it impossible to carry out any baking at all.

The Closeness of Sharing

Life in a Jewish community in Israel, although completely contrary to the situation described by our verse, also facilitates unity among women. In contrast to the western suburban mindset of self-sufficiency, neighbors get together here to use each other's ovens, washing machines, and dryers. When the vegetable market is not just around the corner, the woman next door will be happy to "lend" you a couple of tomatoes, without ever expecting them back. Over the years of living this way, I have come to treasure the closeness of sharing. When we live side by side as one big caring family and build unity among us during times of plenty, with Hashem's help we will not need poverty to teach us this lesson.

The Book of Bemidbar – Wilderness (Numbers)

Parashat Bemidbar

In this week's *parashah* we learn how the camp of Israel had a clearly defined inner structure where everyone knew his place, purpose and mission. "Every man of the children of Israel shall encamp by his own standard, with the signs of their father's house; at some distance around the appointed tent shall they encamp" (*Bemidbar* 2:2).

An Amazing Order

The Jewish people were enumerated and assigned their proper places around the *Mishkan* containing the Holy Ark with the two Torah Tablets. Each tribe was unified under the particular flag which represented it. During the forty years of wandering in the wilderness, Israel encamped according to a precise order around the *Mishkan*. With the ark of Torah as their center, they lifted their eyes towards the point of meeting between the infinite spiritual and the physical boundary. They had a clear understanding that the spiritual must dominate daily physical life in order to sanctify it and allow it to fulfill its purpose.

Surrounding the Ark

Contrary to the western hierarchal linear approach, where the goal is to become "Number One," the tribes of Israel in the wilderness encircled the *Mishkan*. The consciousness and heart of both the nation and the individuals were focused on the center of the camp – the Tent of Testimony. The *Mishkan* was like a mobile Mount Sinai, through which the word of G-d emanated to Moshe. The *Chafetz Chayim* compares the *Mishkan* to the heart. Since the heart generates life, its place is in the middle of the body. This way it disseminates the sustenance contained in the life force of the blood equally to every organ. Israel understood that the Torah is a Tree of Life from which everything derives its nourishment. Just like the Tree of Life was planted in the midst of the Garden (*Bereishit* 2:9); we build the *bimah* (pulpit) in the middle of the synagogue. Thus, we affirm our belief that rather than competing for importance and power, the energy we receive from the Divine source must be circulated equally among us. There is no question about who should be in the front or the back. We all become one when we surround G-d. This concept can be superimposed upon the relationship between men and women. When G-d is in our midst, gender disparities will not turn into competition and conflict. We can overcome power struggles that breaks the circuit and blocks Divine energy from flowing through all of us equally.

Far and Near Are Equally Perfect

"You shall appoint the Levites overseers over *Mishkan* of testimony… and they shall encamp round about the *Mishkan*" (*Bemidbar* 1:50). *Sefat Emet* explains that some people merit perfection by being near the sanctuary while others merit perfection by being far, as it states: "I will create a new expression of the lips. Shalom, shalom (peace/perfection) for [those] far and near, says Hashem" (*Yesha'yahu* 57:19). The common Israelite always had to keep a distance from the place where G-d would reveal Himself, while the Levites were able to come closer. Yet, the other tribes were not jealous of the Levites who in return devoted themselves to the needs of the people. It is interesting to note that the verse actually mentions those who are far first. G-d gives each of us the space that suits our particular nature best. A wise person is someone who knows his place. Israel accepted that whether far or near, when they lived in peace with each other, G-d's Divine Presence dwelled equally among them.

Tuning Into Our Special Space

The boundaries of the camp of Israel teach us that the Divine pattern guides our steps. Every tribe was proud of its individual position within the general community of Israel because this was its proper place for being true to its inner essence. No tribe questioned its particular role. Rather, it was clear that each tribe would complement the others through its particular individuality. Likewise, we have good reason to be proud of our role as women. It is our challenge to delight in womanhood, the way the tribes delighted in their individual roles. Each tribe became dignified by its banner, for it taught them who they really were. Similarly, when we illuminate the special contribution which we impart to the Jewish people as women, we will be able to fill the boundaries of our role with joy.

Parashat Naso

This week's *parashah* tells the unfortunate story of the *sotah* (the woman suspected of adultery). Although her husband warned her against seeing a certain man privately, witnesses, nevertheless, report that she had secluded herself with this particular man. It is not difficult to understand why this act aroused her husband's jealousy. However, since no one had actually witnessed her engaging in the act of adultery, the Torah provides a way of clarifying the matter.

The Unfaithful Wife

In order to clarify whether the husband's jealousy is justified, the Torah instructs him to bring his wife to the *Kohen*, together with a barley offering. The *Kohen* takes holy water from the basin of the *Mishkan* and puts it in an earthen vessel together with some dust from the floor of the *Mishkan*. With this water in his hand, he makes the woman swear that in the case a man other than her husband has lived with her, she accepts, that drinking this water will cause her belly to swell and her thigh to fall away. However, if she has not committed adultery, she is free from the curse of this bitter water, and will conceive a child. "The *Kohen* shall write these curses in a book, and he shall blot them out with the bitter water" (*Bemidbar* 5:23). According to the Talmud (*Sotah* 18a) the words the *Kohen* writes are the description of what the woman swears, which include the name of G-d (*Bemidbar* 5:19–22). After the *Kohen* has read these verses from a parchment and the *sotah* has answered "amen," the parchment is placed in the water and the ink dissolved.

For the Sake of Peace

"Great is shalom between husband and wife, for its sake the Torah permits the name of G-d to become erased" (*Chulin* 141a). The holy Rabbi Meir clearly perceived the depth of this lesson. A certain woman attended his class one night. When she came home, her husband asked her, "Where have you been until now?" She answered, "I was listening to Rabbi Meir teaching." Her husband, in his jealousy, blocked the door saying, "I will not let you in the house until you go and spit in Rabbi Meir's face." Eliyahu the prophet revealed himself to Rabbi Meir and told him the whole story. The Rabbi then went to sit at the Great Synagogue. When the woman came to pray, he made believe that he had an eye ailment. After requesting that she spit seven times in his eye in order to heal him, he told her: "Now, go home and tell your husband, you told me to spit once in Rabbi Meir's face, yet I spat seven times."

Rabbi Meir's students were astonished that he disgraced himself in this way when he could have restored peace between husband and wife in other ways. Why didn't the Rabbi just have her husband beaten up for his abusive behavior? Rabbi Meir answered that if G-d allows His Holy Name to be erased for the sake of *shalom bayit* (peace between husband and wife), how much more so should he be willing to accept disgrace in order to restore *shalom bayit*. G-d, too, could have commanded that the woman be examined without erasing His name. However, G-d taught us in His Torah that it is permitted to erase the name of G-d, for the sake of peace. From this, Rabbi Meir learned not to be concerned about his honor as a Torah scholar, even in a situation where he could have used other means to restore shalom.

G-d's Name is Shalom

"Great is shalom, since all blessings that G-d brings upon Israel culminate in shalom" (*Vayikra Rabbah* 9:9). The Torah is also compared to shalom as it states: "Her ways are ways of pleasantness, and all her paths are peace" (*Mishlei* 3:17). "Rabbi Shimon ben Chalafta said,

Great is shalom, since there is no other receptacle for the blessings, as it states: 'G-d blesses his people with peace' (*Tehillim* 29:11). Even the blessings of the *Kohanim* culminate in shalom, as it states: 'G-d lifts up his countenance to you and gives you peace' (*Bemidbar* 6:26). This teaches us that the blessings have no value unless there is shalom" (*Bemidbar Rabbah* 11:7).

Strife between husband and wife causes the *Shechinah* to depart from Israel. Whenever there is peace between them, the *Shechinah* is with them (*Hanhagat Tzaddikim, Seder Alef Beit*). Therefore, it makes sense that the word Shalom is one of G-d's names. It is actually forbidden to use this word when greeting people in the bathhouse (*Mishnah Berurah* 85:12). We can now understand why restoring peace between husband and wife overrides the prohibition to erase G-d's name. In place of the Divine name erased by the waters of the *sotah*, Shalom – another name for G-d is revealed (Maharal, *Netivot Olam, Netiv HaShalom* 1).

Unifying the Upper and the Lower Worlds

Ohr HaChayim reveals that the importance of shalom derives from the secret of creation, when G-d separated the upper and lower waters. Once the upper waters became the heavens – the dwelling place for the Divine Throne – the lower waters felt left out and cried. G-d wiped their tears and appeased the lower waters with His assurance that the purpose of creating the world is to make a dwelling place for G-d below (*Ohr HaChayim, Bemidbar* 5:15).

A woman suspected of infidelity as a result of secluding herself with another man impairs her own *shalom bayit* thereby refraining from creating a dwelling place for G-d below. In this way, she causes the wailing of the lower waters to reverberate even louder. This explains why the *sotah* is punished through water, and why this water must be taken specifically from the holy *Mishkan*, since its purpose is to unify the upper and lower worlds. Additionally, the barley offering which the *sotah* brings, recalls the sacrifice of Kain, who originally introduced jealousy and strife into the world. The lesson of the *sotah* brings home the importance of dedicating ourselves to promoting shalom in all spheres of life. When we devote our lives to shalom we cause G-d's presence to fill the entire world equally, so that there will no longer be any division between above and below.

Parashat Beha'alotcha

The end of this week's *parashah* recounts how Miriam tried to correct her younger brother Moshe, and help set his relationship with his wife straight. "Miriam and Aharon spoke against Moshe because of the Kushite (Ethiopian) woman, whom he had married, for he had married a Kushite woman" (*Bemidbar* 12:1).

Setting Moshe Rabbeinu Straight

Miriam's words of sisterly advice were considered *lashon hara* (evil speech), although she had the best of intentions – to alleviate the injustice inflicted upon Moshe's wife – she was, nevertheless, afflicted with the plague of leprosy (*Bemidbar* 12:10). Miriam's fate is included in the six remembrances, which we are supposed to recall every day. Why is only Miriam punished when Aharon also spoke together with her? Rashi explains that the name of Miriam is mentioned first in our Torah verse, because she opened the conversation. As the initiator, she had more responsibility for the act.

The Kushite Woman: Black and Beautiful?

Why is Moshe's wife called "the Kushite woman"? According to Rashbam the Kushite woman is a black woman descended from Cham, son of Noach. When Moshe reigned over the Land of Kush for forty years, he married the queen without consummating the marriage. Consequently, Miriam and Aharon criticized him for marrying this Canaanite woman. Ibn Ezra agrees that the Kushite woman is black, but explains that it refers to Tziporah. Although she was from Midian rather than Kush, her skin became black from the abundant sunlight there. Miriam and Aharon suspected that Moshe refrained from living with Tziporah because she was homely. Rashi associates the Kushite woman with Tziporah on opposite grounds. Scripture calls her black to imply that all agreed as to her beauty, just as all agree as to the blackness of an Ethiopian. Moreover, the numerical value of word "Kushite" is the same as that of *yafat mareh* (beautiful of appearance). She was called "the Ethiopian," on account of her beauty, just as a man calls his handsome son "black" in order that the evil eye should have no power over him. However, if the Kushite woman refers to Tziporah, it is not clear why the verse has to inform us "for he had married a Kushite woman," since we already know that Moshe had married Tziporah. Furthermore, regardless of why Tziporah was given the title, "The Kushite Woman," the question still remains as to what fault Miriam and Aharon found in the relationship between Moshe and his wife?

Marital Relations and Prophecy

According to Rabbi S.R. Hirsch the phrase, "for he had married a Kushite woman," does not refer to any woman that Moshe actually married; rather, the expression refers to a marriage without marital relations. Just as it is infeasible for a Jew to marry a black woman who is not Jewish, a marriage without sexual intimacy is regarded as marrying a "Kushite woman." This explanation correlates with the following Midrash quoted by Rashi: Miriam was beside Tziporah when Moshe was told, "...Eldad and Meidad are prophesying in the camp" (*Bemidbar* 11:27). When Tziporah heard this she exclaimed, "Woe to their wives for they will separate from their wives, just as my husband has separated from me!" (Rashi, *Bemidbar* 12:1 based on *Sifrei*). Miriam and Aharon reproved Moshe for using prophecy as a justification for abstaining from marital relations. "They said, Has Hashem indeed spoken only to Moshe? Has He not spoken to us as well?" (*Bemidbar* 12:2). Rabbi S.R. Hirsh explains their claim as follows, since Miriam and Aharon's prophecy did not require them to abstain from marital relationship i.e.

"marry a Kushite woman," why should Moshe's prophecy require him to be separate from his wife? Miriam's well-meant question makes perfect sense in light of the Torah's disapproval of celibacy, as it is taught that the sons of Aharon met their demise for not having fulfilled their obligation to be fruitful and multiply (*Yevamot* 64a). Moreover, Miriam was the midwife of the Jewish people (Rashi, *Shemot* 1:15). Her *raison d'être* was to restore family intimacy for the sake of fulfilling the mitzvah to be fruitful and multiply. Without Miriam, convincing her father to remarry her mother, Moshe would have never been born (Rashi, *Shemot* 2:1). We can, therefore, completely understand how painful it must have been for Miriam to see her little brother seemingly stray from the path to which she had dedicated her life, in order to allow the children of Israel and Moshe himself to be born.

Do Not Judge

According to the *Chafetz Chayim*, the mistake of Miriam and Aharon was judging Moshe by comparing his lifestyle to that of other prophets who did not need to abstain continually from marital relations. Regular prophets abstain from sexual relations only prior to prophecy. Therefore, the entire Jewish people were required to separate from their wives three days prior to receiving the Torah. This is because the seminal discharge of intercourse which causes impurity may possibly continue for three days (see Rashi, *Shemot* 19:15). Yet Moshe's prophecy was on a completely different level than that of all other prophets. As G-d answered Miriam and Aharon, "If there be a prophet among you...My servant Moshe is not so..." (*Bemidbar* 12:6–7). Moshe did not only prophesize occasionally; rather he had to be ready at all times to receive prophecy. Therefore, G-d commanded him to separate from his wife continually.

Mashiach's Wife

In an abstract sense the question still remains as to why the nature of marital relations would interfere with the holiness and special degree of Moshe's prophesy. Will also the Mashiach have to separate from his wife in order to achieve his spiritual purpose? The talmudic statement "A man who has no wife is doomed to an existence without joy, without blessing, without experiencing life's true goodness, without Torah, without protection, and without peace" (*Yevamot* 62b), makes it clear that the relationship with a woman cannot be a distraction that prevents man from achieving his peak of spirituality and communion with G-d.

A person consists of both body and soul. The woman is compared to the body, whereas man is compared to the soul (*Zohar* 1:35a). Chana Weisberg, in *The Crown of Creation*, explains that according to the holy *Zohar*, the essence of the physical existence of the body originates from a higher level of G-dliness than even the spiritual soul. Since the body has descended further from its exalted origin, it is currently on a lower level. In the messianic era, the true essence of the body will be revealed, and the soul will derive spiritual nutrition from the body. Although Mashiach will be the epitome of holiness, he will not be detached from the physical like Moshe, but will have the capability of synthesizing spirituality with materiality. From this we can infer that Mashiach will not have to separate from his wife, as did Moshe. On the contrary, the relationship with his wife will empower him to achieve the ultimate spiritual rectification of all humanity.

Parashat Shelach

In this week's *parashah* the Jewish people are commanded to make an offering to G-d from their bread dough. This offering, which is donated to the *Kohen*, is called *challah*. "When you come into the land where I bring you, then it shall be that when you eat of the bread of the land, you shall offer up an offering unto Hashem. You shall offer up *challah* of the first of your dough for a gift..." (*Bemidbar* 15:18–21).

The Mitzvah of Offering Up Challah

Perhaps the term *challah* has become synonymous with the special bread which we eat on Shabbat because in the spirit of our tradition, the wife of the home bakes her own Shabbat bread and separates off the *challah* offering. According to Beit Hillel, even young unmarried daughters regarded this mitzvah as so important that they would use their own money to bake enough bread to take *challah* every Shabbat eve (*Yoreh Deah* 328). Today, when we don't have the Temple, the mitzvah is performed symbolically by separating a small piece of unbaked dough and burning it or disposing of it respectfully in two bags. According to the *Chazon Ish*, you need to use at least 1 kilos 200 grams (2 lb. 10.2 oz) flour to take *challah* without a *bracha*, and at least 2 kilos 250 grams (4 lb. 15.2 oz) to take *challah* with a *bracha*.

Although this mitzvah is one of the three *mitzvot* designated particularly for women, unfortunately, many ladies today choose to forfeit their special privilege to fulfill the mitzvah of separating *challah*.

When time is sparse, I prefer buying all the other food readymade in order to free myself to perform the important mitzvah of baking homemade *challah*.

Blessings of the Home

The blessings in our homes are closely linked to the mitzvah of taking *challah*. *Sforno* comments that after the sin of the spies the Jewish people needed to bring the *challah* offering in order to be worthy to receive the *bracha* in their homes, as it states: "...you shall also give to the *Kohen* the first of your dough that he may cause a blessing to rest on your home" (*Yechezkel* 44:30). Likewise, Eliyahu told the widow, "...make me a little cake of it first, and bring it to me, afterwards make for you and for your son. For thus says Hashem the G-d of Israel, the jar of meal shall not be spent..." (1 *Melachim* 17:13–14).

There were three special *brachot* (blessings), which returned to the tent of Sarah when Rivkah entered. The light would burn in the tent from one Shabbat eve to the next. There was always a blessing in the dough, and the Cloud of Glory would continually hang over the tent (Rashi, *Bereishit* 24:67). Maharal explains that these three *brachot* derive from the merit of the special *mitzvot* which women perform: The burning light corresponds to lighting the Shabbat candles (*hadlakat nerot*), the Cloud of the Divine Presence to keeping the mitzvah of family purity (*niddah*), and the *bracha* in the dough corresponds to taking *challah* (*Gur Aryeh*, *Bereishit* 24:67). The initials of these three *mitzvot* spell out the name Channah (***Ch**allah*, ***N**iddah*, ***H**adlakat nerot*).

The Sustenance of the Home – In the Merit of the Wife

It might seem logical that the amount of money earned by the household determines the standard of living. Yet the Torah teaches us otherwise. Ultimately, *parnassah* (livelihood) derives from Hashem's blessing. Through the mitzvah of taking *challah*, the wife becomes a worthy vessel for bringing sustenance into her home. The *Yafat Toar* (commenting on *Bereishit Rabbah* 60:16) explains that the particular blessings of the tent of Sarah embody the noble character traits that our mothers possessed. The Cloud of Glory teaches us about their intelligence and spirituality through which they merited the prophetic spirit. The blessing of the continuous candle is a symbol of the *shalom bayit* that they achieved. The blessing in the dough symbolizes being thrifty and careful with the resources. Rather than being a spendthrift in overdraft, the virtuous woman ensures that the most pressing needs of the home are taken care of, before indulging in luxury. "This is the meaning of a *bracha* was always found in her dough" (Rashi, *Bereishit* 24:67).

Rectifying Eating from the Tree of Knowledge

In order to deepen our understanding of why the mitzvah of *challah* causes the blessing of sustenance to enter the home, we need to explore the root of this mitzvah. Our sages (*Yerushalmi, Shabbat* 20a) explain that the three *mitzvot* designated for the Jewish woman enable her to repair the sin of Chava, who brought death into the world by eating from the Tree of Knowledge first. G-d, therefore, gave women the opportunity to bring life into the world through the *mitzvot* of *challah*, lighting the Shabbat candles, and family purity. Humanity is called the bread, candle, and blood of the world, since each of these three *mitzvot* represent another aspect of human life. Mankind is the bread of the world – Hashem shaped man like dough from clay, as it states: "Hashem formed man of the dust of the ground…" (*Bereishit* 2:7). Mankind is the candle of the world as it states: "The candle of G-d, the soul of man…" (*Mishlei* 20:27). Mankind is the blood of the world, as it states: "Whoever spills the blood of man…" (*Bereishit* 9:6). The mitzvah of taking *challah* revitalizes the body, lighting Shabbat candles perfects the soul, while the mitzvah of family purity enables these two opposites to merge. The blood purified through family purity does, in fact, bind body and soul together on a physical level. All of these *mitzvot*, therefore, breathe life into all the aspects of humanity. Since the mitzvah of *challah* brings life into the physical sphere, it follows that keeping this mitzvah is a blessing for livelihood.

Tikun HaOlam (Perfecting the World)

"How is man the *challah* of the world? Just as a woman kneads her dough with water and takes *challah* from it, so, too, 'A mist went up from the earth and watered the whole face of the ground'" (*Bereishit Rabbah* 14:1 quoting *Bereishit* 2:6). Maharal explains that the mitzvah of taking *challah* corresponds to the perfection of the world since the dough, consisting of a mixture of flour and water, is similar to the world which is compound from simple substances. The *challah* being separated out is holy and likened to humanity who is holier than all the other creations. This perfection is alluded to by the fact that human beings were the culmination of the creation process. Likewise the mitzvah of separating *challah* is associated with perfecting the world, since it takes place after the dough is completed (*Chidushei Aggadot* page 145). Perhaps the tradition to braid the *challoth* symbolizes unifying the split consciousness caused by the sin of eating from the Tree of Knowledge of good and evil. There is actually an opinion in the Talmud that the Tree of Knowledge was a wheat tree (*Sanhedrin* 70b). As a result of eating from the Tree, it became dispersed into many sheaves of wheat and its status was lowered into a mere grain. By braiding the *challah*, we symbolically unify the scattered chaffs and elevate them to become one unified *challah*, like the Tree prior to its fall. Whereas it is natural for man to be involved in war and political contention, the innate yearning for peace and harmony embodied by the woman will eventually enable the world to reach perfection. This is why the mitzvah of *challah* is especially designated for the woman.

Parashat Korach

In this week's *parashah* we hear about how the earth opened its mouth and swallowed up Korach, his family and all of his supporters. The cause of this calamity was that Korach, the cousin of Moshe and Aharon, instigated more than two hundred and fifty people to defy the authority of Moshe and the appointment of Aharon as the *Kohen Gadol.*

The Mystery of On Ben Pelet

"Now Korach the son of Yitzhar, the son of Kahat, the son of Levi, and Datan and Aviram, the sons of Eliav, and On the son of Pelet, sons of Reuven, took [men]" (*Bemidbar* 16:1). The son of Pelet is listed as one of Korach's supporters but there is no further mention of him. "Hashem spoke unto Moshe, saying, speak unto the congregation, saying, get you up from about the dwelling of Korach, Datan and Aviram" (*Bemidbar* 16:23–24). On ben Pelet is not included among the people who are punished with Korach. How did he escape sharing their fate?

The Wisdom of Female Charm

In the Talmud (*Sanhedrin* 109b), we find the following anecdote:

> *Rav said, On ben Pelet was saved by his wife. She asked him, "What difference does it make to you whether Moshe or Korach is in charge? In either case, you will be just a student." He answered her, "But what*

can I do? I was in their council and I swore allegiance to them." She replied, "I know that they are all a holy congregation, as it states: 'the entire congregation is holy' (*Bemidbar* 16:3). *Turn back and I will save you." She then served him wine. He got drunk and went to sleep. She went to sit in the doorway of her house, and untied her hair. Whoever saw her went away. [As they didn't want to be exposed to a married woman's uncovered hair]. In the meantime Korach and his supporters were swallowed up.*

According to this Talmud, the wife of On was able to save her husband by understanding that the entire congregation of Israel is so holy and modest that she could be sure that no one would dare to enter their home seeing that her hair was loose. Whoever came to call her husband saw her uncovered hair and retreated (Rashi, *Sanhedrin* 109b).

Korach's Wife

The Talmud continues to explain what caused Korach, a Levite and a *talmid chacham* (Torah scholar), to go against the decree of G-d and thereby cause himself and his supporters to lose both this world and the next.

Korach's wife said to him, "See what Moshe has done, he is the king, his brother has been made Kohen Gadol, and the sons of his brother have been made assistant Kohanim. When people bring terumah (the tithe given to the Kohen), he says, 'give it to the Kohen.' When they bring ma'aser (the tithe given to the Levite), he says, 'give one tenth of it to the Kohen.' Moreover, because he envies you, he has shaven your hair in order to reduce you to a piece of dung." Korach answered, "But he has also shaven his own hair." His wife replied, "It is all for his own advantage. He thinks to himself, 'Let me die with the Pelishtim'" (*Shoftim* 16:30). [*The fact that he himself shaved as well was irrelevant; since he was willing to forgo his own honor, as long as could make everyone else look foolish. In the same way, Shimshon was willing to die as long as he could kill the Pelishtim as well*]. *This is the meaning of, "The wisdom of women builds her house"* (*Mishlei* 14:1);

> *this applies to the wife of On ben Pelet. "...but folly plucks it down with her hands,"* (ibid.) *applies to the wife of Korach.* [*She ignited his suspicion of Moshe, implying that Moshe made up the mitzvah that all Levites must be shaven* (*Bemidbar* 8:7) *in order to make fun of them*] (*Sanhedrin* 110a).

It All Depends on the Woman

The Talmud depicts the great power of womankind by contrasting two influential women. One incited the downfall of Korach and his assembly. The other was able to rescue her husband from the same evil council. What differentiated the ways of these two women whose influence on their husbands had such a tremendous impact on the political and spiritual fate of the entire Jewish nation?

Motivated by the Respect of His Wife

My friend, Shoshanna Lepon, the author of *The Greatest Treasure*, and *Heartbeats* gives the following explanation: A man is motivated by the desire for the respect of his wife. On's wife was interested in building him up. She expressed concern for her husband's esteem when she asked, "What are **you** going to get out of participating in Korach's rebellion?" On's wife was able to persuade her husband by caring about his honor and demonstrating that he had nothing to gain by joining Korach. Korach's wife, on the other hand, related to her husband in precisely the opposite way. Instead of building him up, she put him down and degraded him; making fun of the way he looked after having complied with Moshe's command to shave all his body hair. It was thus Korach's attempt to regain the respect of his wife that incited him to rebel against the authority of Moshe. He wanted to save face and show his wife that he was enough of a man to stand up against Moshe and prevent being made a fool in her eyes.

Looking for the Good

While Korach's wife was critical and always looked for the negative, the wife of On was able to save her husband by looking for the positive element, even within her opponent. The selfsame statement, "...the entire congregation is holy..." (*Bemidbar* 16:3), used by Korach to challenge the authority of Moshe, is turned around by On's wife to acknowledge the virtuous component of Korach and his congregation – the most despicable fragment of the Jewish people. If she was able to perceive the good in the opponents from whom she wanted to protect her husband, how much more can we assume that she constantly looked for the good in her husband? It is this ability to always look for the positive, and build up her husband that the Talmud considers to be "The wisdom of women [which] builds her house."

Parashat Chukat

In this week's *parashah* Miriam departs from this world: "The whole congregation of the children of Israel came into the desert of Zin, in the first month; the people dwelled in Kadesh; Miriam died there, and was buried there. And there was no water for the congregation..." (*Bemidbar* 20:1–2). Why does the lack of water follow immediately after Miriam's death?

In the Merit of Miriam

Rashi explains that during the entire forty years of wandering in the desert the Jewish people was blessed with the well of water in Miriam's merit. His source in the Talmud reads as follows: "Three good providers stood by Israel: Moshe, Aharon and Miriam. Three good gifts were given through them: The manna, the Cloud of Glory, and the well. The well was in the merit of Miriam, the Cloud of Glory in the merit of Aharon, and the manna in the merit of Moshe. When Miriam died, the well subsided; as it states: 'Miriam died there,' followed by, 'there was no water for the congregation'" (*Ta'anit* 9a). Let us try to uncover why the well specifically was in the merit of Miriam. Moreover, is there an underlying connection between women and wells?

The Well of Kindness

According to *Ein Ya'acov*, the three good gifts correspond to the three pillars upon which the world stands: Torah, *avodah* (worship) and *gemilut chassadim* (acts of kindness) (*Pirkei Avot* 1:2). The manna corresponds to Torah, the cloud to worship and the well to acts of kindness. *Anaf Yosef* takes this concept a step further. He explains that just like Miriam embodied the character trait of kindness, when as a young midwife, she kept the babies alive, and supplied them with food (*Shemot* 1:17, see also *Sotah* 11b), so did the well supply the Jewish people with all their needs. Thus, in the merit of Miriam, the well sustained the Jewish people with water in the wilderness. Water symbolizes life, since nothing can grow without it. The nurturing quality of water associated with Miriam is found in womankind. Women keep the world alive. Without the perpetual kindness of women pouring out like a bottomless well, nothing is conceived, born, or kept alive.

Women and Wells

Woman is compared to a well (*Mishlei* 5:15–18). Maharal explains that both rise up from below. The well signifies *hitaruta d'letata* (arousal from below) – the water below the earth, which rise up to the surface. A woman desires her man, because, she yearns for him to draw out her inner depths into the outer reality. This power of the well to rise up is also manifested in the love of the Jewish people for Hashem (*Gevurat Hashem* page 56, *Netzach Yisrael* page 201).

Female Yearning

The desire to always grow, flourish and elevate oneself is clearly expressed among women today. This spiritual female yearning is apparent by the fact that women are in the forefront of the *ba'alei teshuvah* movement (those who return to become observant Jews). It seems that in Jewish learning programs there is often a vast majority of female participants. Moreover, many great teachers prefer female students, because they are more serious in their desire to implement their knowledge. This is also true for various self-development workshops where most participants are women. Women's yearning to ascend on the spiritual ladder paves the way for our future redemption, "...when the earth shall be full of knowledge of Hashem, as the waters covers the sea" (*Yesha'yahu* 11:9).

Parashat Balak

Incited by fear and jealousy, the Moabite King, Balak, hired the Midianite magician, Bilam, to curse the Jewish people. Following multiple attempts of contemporary magic during the most favorable hours, Bilam was unable to curse Israel, since no evil can invade a people dwelling in chastity and holiness.

The Goodly Tents of Ya'acov

"Bilam lifted up his eyes, and he saw Israel dwelling in his tents according to their tribes; and the spirit of Hashem was upon him" (*Bemidbar* 24:2). When Bilam saw how the entrances of the family tents faced away from each other to ensure that no one could peer into the neighbor's tent, he was unable to curse them (Rashi, *Bemidbar* 24:5). Their modesty was totally foreign to the customs of the gentiles and it absolutely fascinated Bilam, to the extent that he could not hold himself back from exclaiming: "How goodly are your tents, O Ya'acov, and your dwellings, O Israel!" (*Bemidbar* 24:5). The woman personifies the tent, which served as the home for the Jewish people during their wandering in the wilderness. Likewise, the name Ya'acov refers to the Jewish women (see Rashi, *Shemot* 19:3).

Modesty – The Guard of Israel's Sanctity

Just imagine how difficult it must have been to preserve a standard of modesty during extended traveling in the wilderness. Privacy is scarce in the cramped conditions of the tent. It took great wisdom for the Israelite women of the tent to guard the modesty and sanctity of her family, under the turbulent lifestyle of camping. Without their creative wisdom how could women take ritual baths, bear children, nurse babies, and tend to hygiene without infringing on the sanctity of modesty which so characterizes the Jewish people? This modesty, surrounding the camp like a hedge of pure white roses, protected Israel from the invasion of any external evil, even the most cunning sorcery. Bilam, however, in his shrewdness, understood the secret of Jewish survival. He discerned that only by making a breach in the hedge of purity surrounding the camp of Israel, would their downfall be near. He, therefore, plotted to arouse the Jewish men with seductive gentile beauties.

The Chaste Jewish Women – "A Fountain Sealed"

"Israel abode in Shittim, and the people began to commit whoredom with the daughters of Moav" (*Bemidbar* 25:1). Rashi informs us that this was by the advice of Bilam. Rabbi S.R. Hirsch notes that the Jewish people never committed harlotry beforehand. Likewise, the Midrash states that during the entire two hundred and ten years of the Egyptian exile, as well as the following forty years of the wandering in the wilderness only one Jewish woman had intimate relations with a gentile (*Midrash Tanchuma, Balak* 16). If it wasn't for Bilam's scheme, the Jews would not suddenly succumb to illicit sexual relations, after having withstood such temptation during the entire Egyptian exile (*Sefer HaMizrachi, Bemidbar* 25:1).

The Tents of Ya'acov – A Faithful Shield

"And the people began to commit whoredom." The Hebrew word used here for "began" is *vayachel* which is related to the word *chol* (profane). By engaging in prohibited sexual relations, the Jewish men profaned their distinctive holiness and began to commit idolatry as well. This is exactly what Scripture warned against, when it forbade intermarriage, as it states: "You take from their daughters to your sons, and their daughters play the harlot after their gods, and make your sons play the harlot after their gods" (*Shemot* 34:16). Sexual chastity, therefore, protects the Jewish people from every negative influence. As long as the men of Israel were under the faithful shield of their Jewish women – the guardians of the goodly tents of Ya'acov – no evil could befall them. However, as soon as they left their tents, to go astray after strange women, they made themselves vulnerable to every conceivable sin, including idol worship. After breaching the protective shield of the tent, *B'nei Yisrael* (the children of Israel) became victims to the curse of anti-Semitism, and twenty-four thousand people lost their lives. Here, again, is an example of how the survival of Israel depends on the merit of the Jewish women.

Parashat Pinchas

"Then approached the daughters of Tzelafchad, the son of Chefer, the son of Gilead, the son of Machir, the son of Menasheh, of the families of Menasheh the son of Yosef; and these are the names of his daughters; Machlah, Noah, Choglah, Milkah, and Tirtzah…saying… 'Wherefore should the name of our father be done away from among his family, because he had no son? Give unto us, therefore, a possession among the brothers of our father'" (*Bemidbar* 27:1–4).

Among These There Was No Man

The request of the five brave daughters of Tzelafchad for an inheritance in Israel follows immediately after the Torah's account of how Kalev and Yehoshua were the only men who left Egypt that merited to enter the Land of Israel, as it states: "…among these there was no man…" (*Bemidbar* 26:64). Commenting on this juxtaposition, Rashi explains that the decree resulting from the incident of the spies had not been enacted upon the women, because they held the Promised Land dear. The men had said, "Let us appoint a chief and return to Egypt" while the women desired "a possession in the land." Likewise, Malbim asserts that the women in that generation were on a higher level than the men. Menachem Becker points out that Hashem never commanded Moshe to send male spies. Rashi commented on the beginning of *Parashat Shelach*, "'Send for yourself…' i.e. according to your own judgment. I do not command you, but if you wish to do so, send them." Later sages have explained this Rashi in the following manner: I would have suggested that you send women to spy the land, for they would not speak evil about it, but if you decide to send men, behold, that is on your own responsibility (*Parparaot l'Torah*, *Parashat Pinchas*).

Between Comfort and Devotion

"Of the families of Menasheh the son of Yosef" Malbim asks why it was necessary to mention Yosef in connection with Tzelafchad's daughters? Since Scripture states that they are from the tribe of Menasheh, it follows that they are descended from Yosef as well. He explains that half of the tribe of Menasheh received their heritage on the other side of the Jordan River because they did not hold the Land of Israel dear. However, the daughters of Tzelafchad were associated with Yosef in their love of the Land of Israel. Yosef expressed his love of Israel by requesting that his brothers swear to bring his bones up to the Holy Land. Similarly, the daughters of Tzelafchad requested a portion within the land and asked: "Give us a possession among the brothers of our father." Their father's brothers were the sons of Chefer, whose lots were inside of Israel proper. Although the grass was greener, and life seemed easier on the other side of the Jordan River, the daughters of Tzelafchad were not enticed by easy comforts. The heroines of our *parashah* were not interested in just making a living off the land. They wanted a part in the spiritual promise of cultivating a relationship with G-d through the land – the physical vehicle for revealing Hashem's blessing in the world. Today, when we are similarly faced with the challenge to choose between comfort and idealism, the daughters of Tzelafchad serve as an eternal inspiration.

Women Excel in Emunah

If possession of the land depended solely on conquest in war, it would have been fair to allot it only to those who endangered their lives in warfare. Women would then be undeserving of a portion, since it isn't the custom for women to engage in war. The daughters of Tzelafchad realized that the Jewish people already had the right to the land through the eternal merit of Avraham who had conquered it in a spiritual sense for all his descendants. The men, who said, "…let us appoint a chief to return to Egypt" (*Bemidbar* 14:4), lacked faith in their ability to possess the land through the merit of their forefathers. They failed to understand that the land had already been sanctified through G-d's promise to Avraham, which made it possible for Israel to conquer it (*Chatam Sofer, Bereishit* 14:4). When we don't rely on our own strength, our faith can remain steadfast even if the task seems beyond our capability. Perhaps the reason that women have a greater connection with the Land of Israel is that we excel in *emunah*, and are less inclined to rely on our own strength.

The Daughters of Tzelafchad Teach Halachah

"The chapter [regarding the laws of women inheriting land] ought to have been taught in the name of Moshe, but because the daughters of Tzelafchad had so much merit, it was written through them" (*Baba Batra* 119a, *Sanhedrin* 8a). Rabbi Eliyahu Kitov asks, what was the great merit of Tzelafchad's daughters that they taught laws of Torah, which even Moshe was unable to teach? He explains that they arose in the generation of the wilderness and merited receiving the reward for the entire generation. Moshe asked them, "Behold, Israel wants to return to Egypt, and you request an inheritance in the land?" They answered, "We know that in the end, Israel will possess the land." This is what Hillel used to say, "In a place where nobody jumps at the merchandise, buy it; in a place where there are no men, become a man" (*Pirkei Avot* 2:5). Even at a time when everyone had lost hope, the request of the daughters of Tzelafchad showed their tremendous faith and conviction that the people of Israel would return to its borders. This is the special *zechut* through which the daughters merited to reveal a portion of the Torah; as Rashi states regarding the verse, "the daughters of Tzelafchad speak right…" (*Bemidbar* 27:7). This tells us that their eye saw what Moshe's eye did not see (Rashi, ibid.). The daughters of Tzelafchad had so much merit that they experienced an even finer perception of certain parts of the Torah than Moshe himself.

Parashat Matot

Parashat Matot teaches us that if a woman makes a vow, taking upon herself a particular stringency, her father may annul it so she will no longer be bound by it. "But if her father disallow her in the day that he hears, not any of her vows, or of her bonds, wherewith she has bound her soul, shall stand; and Hashem shall forgive her, because her father disallowed her" (*Bemidbar* 30:6). When she marries, her husband will be empowered to nullify her vow instead. "Every vow, and every binding oath to afflict the soul, her husband may establish it, or her husband may make it void" (ibid. 14).

Seemingly Chauvinistic Laws

How do we explain the fact that a man can nullify a vow taken by his daughter or wife, whereas a woman cannot nullify any vow taken by her son or husband? On the surface level, it seems as though the Torah denigrates woman by regarding her as unable to take responsibility for her own decisions. Although we acknowledge the Divine source of all Torah laws, how can we, as mature liberated women, accept laws which seem to limit our independence?

Eternal Laws of Torah Outweigh Norms of Modern Society

Whenever Torah laws contradict what is socially acceptable in the "free" western world, the eternal value of the Torah takes precedence over the ephemeral values of the western world. However, there is a reason why

Hashem causes certain perspectives to become more popular at certain times. Each wave of consciousness draws out another aspect contained within the depths of the wellsprings of Torah. Our need to affirm the importance of women in Judaism becomes an impetus for perceiving the Torah laws that seem to belittle women's role in a deeper way.

Achieving Divine Forgiveness

According to Torah law any vow taken is binding, and cannot easily be dismissed. Today, therefore, it is the custom never to make any vow in case we accidentally should come to transgress it. The *Kol Nidrei* prayer on Yom Kippur comes to nullify any vows that we may not have fulfilled. Only then can we receive forgiveness for unfulfilled vows even if our inability to keep them was unintentional. Commenting on the phrase "Hashem shall forgive her," Rashi ponders why the woman needs forgiveness, when her vow has already been annulled. He explains that Scripture describes the case of a woman who vowed to become a Nazarite and whose father heard it and annulled it for her without her knowledge. Even though her vow was void, she thought it was still in effect. Therefore, she needed forgiveness when acting contrary to the vow she had taken upon herself. Rashi points out that by revoking the vow of the daughter or wife, she is able to merit forgiveness in case she should accidentally break it. His comment concludes with a fortiori: If those whose vows have been annulled require forgiveness, how much more when someone transgresses vows which have not been annulled. (Rashi, *Bemidbar* 30:6).

For the Sake of Protecting the Woman

Although nullifying the woman's vow removes the punishment, should she be unable to fulfill it; this does not prevent her from carrying out what she has sworn. Let's say a woman takes upon herself to become a vegetarian. The ability to annul her vow does not give her husband the power to force her to eat meat. It only prevents her from being punished, should she accidentally come to eat meat. Moreover, not every vow can be nullified by her father or husband. Rabbi S.R. Hirsch explains that the right of the husband to annul her vow is limited to the vows through which the woman causes herself hardship and pain, or vows that pertain to their relationship. Thus, the ability to annul her vow serves as a protection for the woman. Since according to Rabbi Ezriel Tauber's analogy, the woman is compared to a diamond, (see our teaching on *Parashat Vayislach* on page 27), she needs this additional protection because of her great value.

Women, Sensitivity, and Self Sacrifice

All generalizations have their exceptions. It is especially difficult in our evolving world, to describe prototypes of men and women. Nevertheless, the fact that men and women are created with physical differences alludes to their different emotional and spiritual makeup; since everything in the physical world is a reflection of the spiritual reality it manifests. Whereas it is generally easier for a man to be detached and objective, a woman's role as a nurturer of new life makes her more emotionally sensitive, enabling her to love and identify with others. In her selflessness and zeal to give, she might not always realize her own limitations. A woman could, therefore, easily come to take upon herself more than she can handle. Her husband's ability to annul her vow serves to prevent her altruistic nature from going overboard.

Men Need to Protect

As much as a woman needs to be protected, all the more, a man needs to protect. It is the moral strength of a woman that enables her to give her man a feeling of importance by seeking refuge under his protective shield. As John Gray writes in *Men are from Mars, Women are from Venus*, "Deep inside, every man wants to be his woman's hero or knight in shining armor." Women have enough inner confidence to allow men to have the last word. In various circumstances, the primary role of the man is one of decision making whereas that of the woman is motivating and encouraging her man. In the overall picture, both are equally responsible for the final decisions, in the same way that both have an equal share in shaping the baby that the woman bears.

Parashat Masei

In our day and time, there is an intensified awareness of the inherent holiness of the Land of Israel, especially among women. In spite of current difficulties, our attachment to the Land of Israel is constantly being strengthened as we expand and build new communities in the land. Today's righteous women have reawakened the bond shared with the eternal dwelling place of Rachel our Mother, who is buried in Beitlechem. Likewise, in Chevron, the burial site of our patriarchs and matriarchs, women steadfastly ensure that this holy city remains in the hands of Israel. In their great faith, the women of Gush Katif (Gaza) sowed vegetable crops for the coming season, in spite of the looming threat of expulsion from the land where they had taken root.

Redeeming the Land

From where do women get the strength to stand up for the land despite the dangers this entails? The deeds of the fathers [and mothers] affect their children (Ramban, *Bereishit* 12:6). We are only an extension of the souls that preceded us. The spiritual rectifications of our ancestors pave the way for our continued efforts. Among the role models that have affected our inherent attachment to the Land of Israel are the daughters of Tzelafchad. At a time when the general sentiment of love for the Land of Israel was remiss, these five sisters stood out in their yearning and dedication to redeem their portion of the Land of Israel with the intention to reveal the *Shechinah*. Their spirit strengthens and propels our endeavor to reclaim our Holy Land.

Within Their Tribe

It is not clear whether the daughters of Tzelafchad were permitted to marry whoever they wanted or whether they were commanded to marry only within their own tribe:

> *"This is the thing which Hashem commands concerning the daughters of Tzelafchad, saying, let them marry whom they think best; only within the family of the tribe of their father shall they marry. So the inheritance of the children of Israel shall not be removed from tribe to tribe…"* (*Bemidbar* 36:6–7). *Shemuel said, the daughters of Tzelafchad were permitted to marry all the tribes as it states: "…let them marry whom they think best." So how can we understand, "… only within the family of the tribe of their father shall they marry"? Scripture gave them the good advice that they should only marry those who are fitting for them* (*Baba Batra* 120a).

The daughters of Tzelafchad had full permission to choose a marriage partner outside of their own tribe. However, in order to ensure that the land would not be lost permanently from their tribe, they were advised to marry within the tribe. The Talmud praises Tzelafchad's daughters' willingness to wait in order to find suitable marriage partners within their own tribe in order to redeem the land. "They were righteous since they did not marry except those who were fitting for them. Rabbi Eliezer ben Ya'acov taught, even the youngest among them did not marry before she turned forty…" (Ibid. 119b).

Righteous Petition

Petitions and requests are often colored by self interest. We may not be aware that our idealistic words sometimes are rationalizations for egocentric desires. Tzelafchad's daughters requested an inheritance for the sake of the continuation of their father's name. They desired to redeem the land belonging to their father in order that his soul should have an eternal physical manifestation. Had they then married men from other tribes, their father's land would have passed from his eternal spiritual possession as a member of the tribe to the property of the tribe of their husbands. In that case, their request, "Why should the name of our father be done away with..." (*Bemidbar* 27:4), would merely have been a rationalization for their personal desire to acquire land. Their willingness to wait until they found a suitable husband within their tribe, all the while risking becoming too old for childbearing, proved that the intention of their petition was completely altruistic.

Only for That Generation

The land derives its spiritual mission from the tribe that originally inherited each particular lot. The tribes infused their soul into the portion of land allotted to them, shaping the land according to the Divine design. Rabbi S.R. Hirsch explains the importance that every tribe takes root in its designated land, ensuring the characteristics and individuality of each tribe. However, this must not detract from the importance of the unity among all the tribes when surrounding the *Mishkan*. For this reason, the advice to the daughters to marry within their own tribe only pertained to their generation. If not so, a situation of apartheid between the tribes could have been created. After the conquest of the Land of Israel, when the outline of each tribe had become established, it was no longer a problem if a daughter would inherit and transfer her portion to the tribe of her husband. *Ba'al HaTurim* brings further support for this point from Scripture: "This is the thing..." (*Bemidbar* 36:6) has the same numerical value as "in that generation."

Women Reveal the Shechinah in the Land

The incident of the daughters of Tzelafchad occurs on the last stage of the forty-two stage journey from Egypt to the Holy Land. Its re-enactment in the six thousand year scale of history will be one of the last developments before the final messianic age. We are now collectively at, or very close to, the "plains of Moav" about to enter the Land of Israel; and the glow of its dawning light is certainly present. It is therefore no surprise that a growing number of women in this generation identify with the daughters of Tzelafchad and find their own stories, dilemmas, and yearnings mirrored in their tale.

> *When the daughters of Tzelafchad heard that the land was being divided among the tribes but not to the women, they convened to discuss the matter. They said, "G-d's mercy and compassion is not like the compassion of mankind. Mankind favors men over women. G-d is not that way; his compassion is on men and women alike. He has mercy on all, as it states: 'Hashem is good to all and His mercy is upon all His deeds…'"* (*Sifri*, *Pinchas* 2 quoting *Tehillim* 145:9)

Sarah Yehudit Schneider explains that the daughters of Tzelafchad understood that as long as the *Shechinah* remains in exile, women will be suppressed and the land will remain unredeemed. They identified with the pain of the exiled Feminine Indwelling Presence and stood up for their rights as women, in order to redeem the land and reveal the *Shechinah* on earth. The story of the daughters of Tzelafchad, along with the laws of inheritance of the land that concludes the traveling in the desert and the book of *Bemidbar* will be the final destiny of our own journeys as well. It alludes to the fact that the final *geulah* (redemption) will be brought about by righteous women who are willing to employ self-sacrifice and take risks in order to attach themselves to the Land of Israel and reveal its innate holiness.

The Book of Devarim – Words (Deuteronomy)

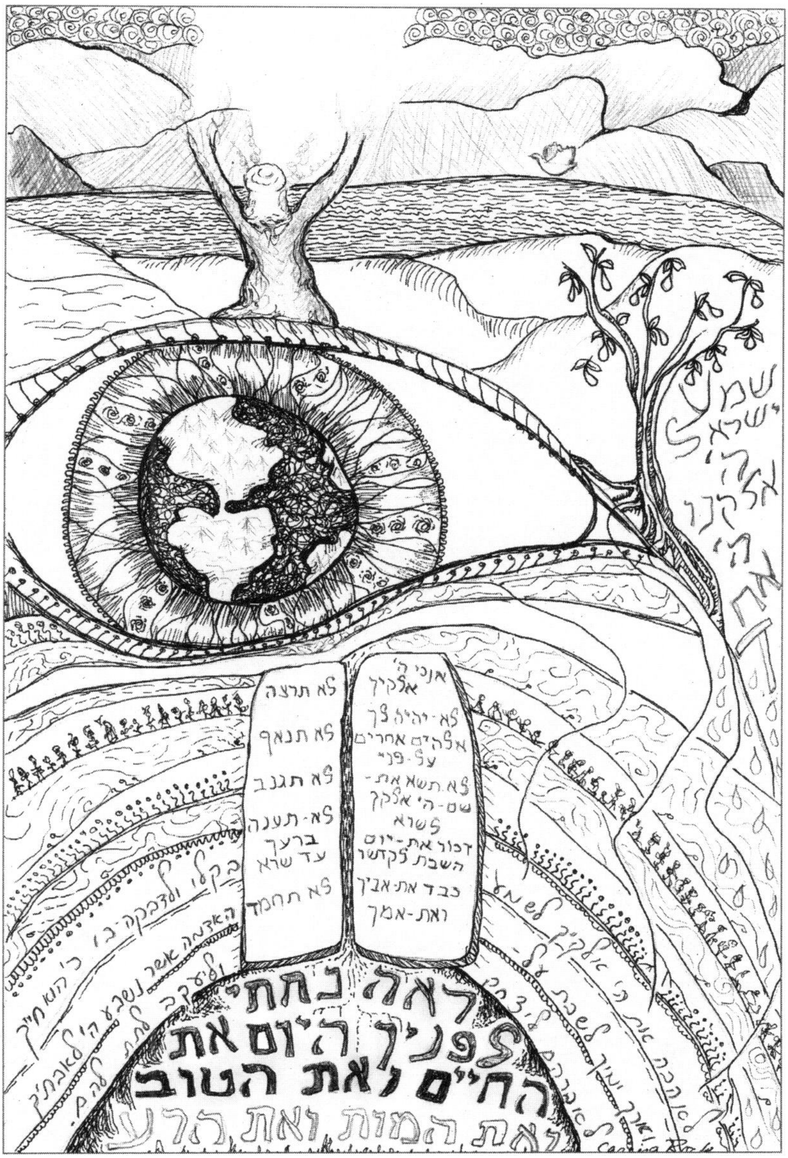

Parashat Devarim

The importance of placing the wife before anyone, including the children, is hinted in this week's *parashah*: "Hashem your G-d has given you this land to possess it...but your wives, and your little ones, and your cattle...shall abide in your cities which I have given you" (*Devarim* 3:18–19). These are Moshe's subtle words of rebuke to the tribes of Reuven and Gad who originally requested land on the other side of the Jordan River saying, "...we will build sheepfolds here for our cattle, and cities for our little ones" (*Bemidbar* 32:16). Moshe then reversed the order adjusting their words as follows: "Build cities for your little ones and folds for your flock" (ibid. 32:24).

A Question of Priorities

According to Rashi, the tribes of Reuven and Gad mentioned their cattle before their children because they paid more regard to their property than to their sons and daughters. Moshe told them, keep your priorities correct. First build cities for your little ones and afterwards folds for your flock. They accepted Moshe's rebuke and corrected themselves saying: "Our little ones, our wives, our cattle, and all our beast shall be there in the cities of Gilead" (*Bemidbar* 32:26). Yet, their proposal still needed fine tuning, since they placed their children before their wives. Therefore, Moshe now mentions the wives first on the list, in order to make them aware that no one takes precedence over their spouse.

Alone Together

Although our children are most precious to us, representing our future continuation, no one is as close to the other as husband and wife. "That is why man leaves his father and his mother, and cleaves to his wife and they become one flesh" (*Bereishit* 2:24). The unity between husband and wife is intrinsically linked to the original intention of creation: "Male and female He created them" (*Bereishit* 1:27).

> *From here we learn, any image that does not embrace male and female is not a high and true image…Come and see, the blessed Holy One does not place His abode in any place where male and female are not found together. Blessings are found only in a place where male and female are found, as it is written: "He blessed them and called* ***their*** *name Adam on the day they were created" (Bereishit 5:2). It is not written; He blessed him and called* ***his*** *name Adam. A human being is only called Adam when male and female are as one* (*Zohar* 1:55b).

Your Wives Take Precedence

G-d could have ingrained within nature the arrival of offspring from the beginning of marital union. He could have made the woman conceive, and give birth on the same day. Yet, it is Hashem's desire that man and woman spend a substantial amount of time alone together without the distraction of the brood. Therefore, husband and wife live at least nine months alone together before little ones enter their nest. Moreover, children are meant to grow up, leave the nest and start their own families. In this natural process of unfolding life, husband and wife are again left to themselves. Therefore, Moshe makes it clear to the men that just like their children are more important than their career, so are their wives most important of all.

Parashat Va'etchanan

The issue of "who is a Jew?" arouses much debate. In the wake of numerous immigrants entering Israel, the subject has taken on new relevance, since many of them are intermarried. Naturally, people who have been persecuted due to their Jewish ancestry feel the right to enjoy the privileges of being Jewish as well.

Who is a Jew?

Not everyone is ready to accept that the Jewish lineage depends solely on the mother, and that according to Halachah a child born to a gentile mother is not considered Jewish, even if the father is Jewish. The popular explanation that only the identity of the mother can be ascertained is no longer valid in our time, since the identity of the father can now be verified through genetic tests.

The Son of a Gentile Mother

The Scriptural source for the law of "who is a Jew?" is found in this week's *parashah*: "Neither shall you intermarry with them; your daughter you shall not give unto his son, nor his daughter shall you take unto your son. For he will turn away your son from following Me, and they may serve other gods…" (*Devarim* 7:3–4). Scripture speaks here of two cases of intermarriage:

1. A Jewess becomes the wife of a gentile.
2. A Jew becomes the husband of a gentile woman.

It is not quite clear from the verse who will be the one to turn the other away from following G-d. If the verse referred to the negative influence of the non-Jewish party over his/her Jewish spouse, then we would expect two parallel statements expressing the reason for the prohibition.

1. "For he will turn away your daughter from following Me."
2. "For she will turn away your son from following Me."

Yet, Scripture mentions neither of these two cases, stating only the following unexpected third possibility: "For he will turn away your son from following Me." Rashi explains that "he" refers to the gentile husband of the Jewess. Who then is "your son" that this gentile man may turn away from following Hashem? Based on the fact that grandchildren are often called children in Scripture (see Rashi, *Bereishit* 20:12), Rashi explains that "your son" refers to your grandson, the son of your daughter, who is at risk of being turned away from the Torah path by his non-Jewish father. This teaches us that only the son of a Jewess and a gentile father is called "your son," but the son of a non-Jewish mother with a Jewish father is not defined as your son. Therefore, in regards to the statement, "...his daughter you shall not take to your son," it does not add, "for she will turn away your son from following Me." Scripture does not consider the son of this gentile mother "your son" because he does not belong by birth to the Jewish people. The Halachah follows Rashi's explanation which is supported by the Talmud stating, "The son from a Jewish mother is called your son, but the son from a gentile mother is not called your son" (*Kiddushin* 68b). Based on this source, Rambam establishes as Halachah that a child born of a gentile woman is not considered Jewish (*Mishneh Torah*, Prohibited Relationships 12:7).

The Mother Gives Over Her Essence

How do we explain the fact that only the mother determines the Jewishness of her children? Which magic power does the mother have to influence her children more than the father? Rabbeinu Bachaya on *Bereishit* 29:25 explains that the mother gives over her essence to her offspring. This is why it was the matriarchs who named their children, as the name expresses a person's essence. Rachel's children inherited her craft of silence. When Ya'acov sent her gifts, Lavan took them and gave them to Leah, yet Rachel remained silent. Therefore, all her children were masters of silence. Binyamin, the son of Rachel, knew that Yosef was sold, but kept silent. Esther, from the tribe of Binyamin, son of Rachel, did not reveal the identity of her people (*Megillah* 13b). Leah was the master of the craft of thanksgiving and praise (*hodayah*). Therefore, all her children were masters of *hodayah*, as it states: "Yehudah, your brothers shall praise you (*yoducha*)" (*Bereishit* 49:8). David, her descendant, said, "Give thanks (*hodu*) to Hashem…" (*Tehillim* 136:1).

A Space Within Her

The *Imrei Shefer* compares the womb, to the *mikvah*, which has the capacity to convert a person to Judaism. He explains that the mother determines the spiritual genetics of the Jewish people because of the great impact the womb has on the unborn child. The fact that the mother carries the baby within her reveals her capacity to carry on the Jewish lineage. The mother is characterized as one who makes space within herself for another being to grow. This ultimate kindness, which continues throughout the role of motherhood, can be compared to the way G-d created the world. In order to allow the existence of the Universe, G-d, so to speak, had to constrict His own essence and make space for something other than Himself. This is the secret of the *tzimtzum* (constriction) explained by our kabbalistic masters. When pouring wine out from a glass, a *reshimo* (residue) adheres to the glass. Likewise, when G-d made space within Himself, a drop of Divinity remained within the vacuum. This imprint affects G-d's creation and imbues it with His essence. By sacrificing her own personal space for the sake of her unborn baby, the mother imparts her essence to her offspring in the same way that G-d, by constricting Himself, imparts His essence to mankind – the crown of His creation. This explains why the mother is the carrier of the Jewish lineage.

Parashat Eikev

Parashat Eikev describes the blessings that G-d bestows upon the Jewish people when we keep the *mitzvot*. The first blessing mentioned is the blessing of begetting children: "…if you listen to these judgments, keep, and do them, that Hashem your G-d shall keep for you the covenant and the loving/kindness which He swore to your fathers. He will love you and bless you, multiply you; and bless the fruit of your womb" (*Devarim* 7:12–13).

The Blessings of the Fruit of the Womb

Israel's blessing of fertility is certainly being fulfilled as we witness Torah observant families as replete with little ones, as clusters of grapes filling a fruit basket. The Torah continues to elaborate on this blessing, "You shall be blessed above all peoples, there shall not be male or female barren among you, or among your animals" (*Devarim* 7:14). In our day and time we are witnessing the partial fulfillment of this blessing of fertility, as modern medicine develops new techniques for overcoming infertility. However, we pray that this blessing will continue to flourish and affect all the barren women of Israel, since many couples still suffer from childlessness.

Prayer and Human Effort Go Hand in Hand

No matter how developed the modern approaches for overcoming infertility are, prayer continues to be the most vital component of begetting children. However, we are also required to exert *histadlut* (human effort) and use whatever means available today to accomplish the goal of conception, pregnancy and birth. In this way, prayer and medical procedures go hand in hand. The word for barren in Hebrew is *akar*, which also means "to uproot" or "eradicate." Thus, the *Shach* reads our verse as follows: "[The prayer of] male or female will never **be uprooted** among you or among your animals." What is the connection between the word *akar*, and "your animals"? The *Shach* explains, when people humble themselves like the animals of the field, depending on G-d for survival, then their prayer will never be uprooted but remain before G-d for eternity.

Revealing G-d's Miracles Within Procreation

Malbim writes that although the success of the nations is bound by the laws of nature that do not preclude the existence of infertility, the Jewish people is an exception. Albeit, contrary to the way of nature, there will come a time when no one will be barren among Israel. It may seem that modern society's interaction with the process of creation through scientific medical procedures such as In-Vitro Fertilization (IVF) diminishes the Divine miracle of creation. With so much power and ability to interfere with the natural reproductive process, it may appear as if humanity is trying to play G-d without acknowledging the need for Divine assistance. This does not have to be true. Artificial insemination may actually heighten our awareness of the Divine blessings necessary to produce a child. In spite of advanced technology, no expert can predict which ovum will be fertilized to become an embryo, or explain why only certain embryos become implanted in the womb and only some of them grow, while others are expelled. Each stage of creation needs the blessing of G-d to succeed.

During natural conception, one may take the miraculous process of preganancy for granted due to lack of awareness of what it takes to create a healthy baby. The IVF process makes it possible to closely follow each of the steps, heightening the awareness of the Divine miraculous creation. What usually takes place "naturally" concealed within the womb is now brought out into consciousness. Through our interaction with nature, the complicated miracle of creating an infant is revealed, making us tremble, hope, and pray for the success of each stage. May G-d hearken to our prayers, and remember all the barren women of Israel with the blessing of the fruit of their womb!

Parashat Re'eh

"You shall rejoice in your festival, you and your son, your daughter, your servant, your maidservant, the Levite, the stranger, the fatherless, and the widow, that are within your gates" (*Devarim* 16:14). "Rejoicing in your festival" comprises a celebration in Jerusalem, partaking of the sacrifices brought to the Temple. Our sages teach that women are also obligated to rejoice in the peace offerings of joy (*Mishnah Berurah* 529:15).

Rejoicing for the Sake of G-d

According to *Sefer HaChinuch* (Mitzvah 488), rejoicing includes drinking wine, dressing up in new clothes, giving out fruits and candies to the children, playing music and singing in Jerusalem. The root of the mitzvah is that people need to celebrate periodically in the same way that we need food, rest, and sleep. G-d desired that we dedicate this joy to His name, in order to increase our merits that we may find favor before Him. Therefore, He established the pilgrim festivals to remember the miracles and the goodness, which He bestows upon us. At these times, we fulfill Hashem's mitzvah by nourishing our physical needs, celebrating with the good things of life, and acknowledging our Ultimate Provider. When our satisfaction and happiness are for the sake of G-d, we are assured that our joy will remain within the boundaries of what is proper, without going overboard and becoming licentious.

Rejoicing in Our Wrappings

Rambam explains that each person needs to rejoice in the way most appropriate for him or her. He notes that children enjoy nuts and sweets; men primarily become happy through eating meat and drinking wine; whereas women delight in wearing new clothing and jewelry (*Mishneh Torah*, The Laws of Holidays 6:18). In suggesting the different ways men and women achieve happiness; our sages demonstrate their perception of the fundamental difference between them. Let us try to tune into the question of why men rejoice through wine and women through beautiful clothes. The physical is always an outward manifestation of the inner spiritual reality. As known from the physiological differences between men and women, and from the creation of woman from inside of man (*Bereishit* 2:23); women are primarily internal, whereas men are primarily external beings. (See also our quote from Prayer and Destiny on page 191). True happiness is to achieve perfect balance by completing ourselves. Therefore, it makes sense that men who are primarily external find happiness through something internal, whereas women who are primarily internal rejoice in their external wrappings.

Appearance as a Way of Self Expression

"When wine goes in, the secrets come out" (*Eruvin* 65b). Wine helps expressing our innermost thoughts and feelings. When men get moody, they often withdraw and refuse to express their feelings. John Gray writes in *Men are from Mars, Women are from Venus*: "When a man is stressed he will withdraw into the cave of his mind and focus on solving a problem…at such times, he becomes increasingly distant, forgetful, unresponsive, and preoccupied in his relationships…" It is certainly possible that a little wine can help a man come out of his "cave," express his inner feelings and get relief from his emotional isolation. Then, he will be able to relate to his wife, and thus find ultimate happiness. A woman does not have the same difficulty expressing herself verbally. She actually loves to express herself, both through her words and appearance. It is important for her to be adored by her man, as John Gray writes, "A woman thrives when she feels adored and special. A man fulfills her need to be loved when he makes her feelings and needs more important than his other interests..." By accentuating her beauty through her mode of dress, she not only enjoys expressing herself, but is also better able to attract the attention of her man.

A Beautiful Garment for Her Soul

Women are drawn to beauty and harmony. Therefore, we delight in beautiful garments. Just as wine helps a man bring out his thoughts and express himself, similarly, through her clothing, a woman expresses the creativity of her soul. The halachic requirement for man to wear a belt when he prays to Hashem indicates that men are required to make a conscious separation between their upper spiritual soul and lower physical body (*Shulchan Aruch, Orach Chayim* 91:2). However, a woman's body is a much more refined garment for her soul. This is reflected in the beautiful dresses with which she wraps her body that becomes an extension of her spirit. Therefore, no division is necessary. Nice clothes make her happy, because they enable her to beautify and express her innermost being.

The Beauty of Simplicity and the Women of the Land

In the discussion in the Talmud regarding the kinds of clothing that make women happy, Rabbi Yosef relates that the women of Babylon enjoy multicolored garments; whereas the women of the Land of Israel prefer clothes made of white, ironed linen (*Pesachim* 109a). Representing those who are in exile, the women of Babylon express themselves in fancy, multicolored robes. In contrast, the women of the Land of Israel are happy to cover themselves with simple white linen dresses. From my experience living both in exile and in Israel, I have noticed that this difference of attire is still in effect. Multicolored fancy garments are an expression of the fragmentation of exile, whereas the closeness to the One and only G-d in Israel is expressed through simplicity. The color white derives from blending all the colors in perfect harmony, letting the light shine through each of them equally. Therefore, in the Land of Israel, women do not need fancy garments to impress or surpass anyone. Our unity with each other and Hashem can be expressed through simplicity.

Parashat Shoftim

"Shalom" is the red thread that ties this week's *parashah* together, as Rabbeinu Bachaya writes in his introduction to *Parashat Shoftim*. The Torah commands us to appoint judges in order to bring shalom to the world and uphold its existence.

Appoint Judges to Prevent War

"Judges and officers shall you make for you in all your gates, which Hashem your G-d gives you, throughout your tribes, and they shall judge the people with righteous judgment" (*Devarim* 16:18). If not for maintaining justice, people would have stolen and killed each other to the point where the world would have been unable to endure. Acting in accordance with Hashem's command and His appointed leaders enables us to eradicate evil from the world. This is the way to bring the redemption closer, a time when all warfare will be extinguished. As the prophet promises, "He shall judge among the nations, and shall decide among many people, and they shall beat their swords into plowshares and their spears into pruning hooks, nation shall not lift up sword against nation, neither shall they learn war anymore" (*Yesha'yahu* 2:4).

A Chance for All to Make Peace

Parashat Shoftim teaches us the greatness of shalom through the mitzvah of giving our enemies a chance to surrender and make peace before engaging in war: "When you approach a city to fight against it, then proclaim peace unto it" (*Devarim* 20:10). Rabbeinu Bachaya explains that the mitzvah of offering the enemy nation a chance to make peace applies to any city and any kind of war including a war that Hashem commands us to wage (*milchemet mitzvah*), with the exception of the war against the nations of Ammon and Moav about whom it states, "...do not seek their peace" (ibid. 23:7). However, if they offer to make peace on their own initiative, we accept it even from them. "See how great is the power of peace, that we are required to extend it even to those who hate G-d" (*Midrash Tanchuma, Shoftim* 18). From the verse, "There was not a city that made peace with the children of Israel, except for the Chivi, who dwelled in Givon..." (*Yehoshua* 11:19), it is understood that Yehoshua (the leader of Israel) gave all the people a chance to make peace, but they refused.

Greater Than Truth

For the sake of shalom it is of uttermost importance that all Israel is united under the authority of their judges. "According to the Torah that they shall teach you, and according to the judgment that they shall tell you, you shall do. You shall not deviate from the Torah that they shall tell you, to the right or to the left" (*Devarim* 17:11). Rashi comments that you must follow the judge, even if he tells you that right is left and that left is right. How much more so if he says that right is right and left is left. This teaches us that we are expected to compromise truth for the sake of peace. Similarly, *Sefer HaChinuch* concludes that we are required to follow our sages even when they make a mistake. For it is better to suffer one mistake and surrender to the authority of their great knowledge, than to have each individual act according to what is straight in his own eyes. We are likewise required to extend the principle, "Peace is greater than truth" for the sake of *shalom bayit* between husband and wife. Thus, when G-d addressed Avraham, He changed the words of Sarah, to prevent any bad feelings from arising between them (see our teaching on *Parashat Vayera* on page 15).

All is Completed in Shalom

Maharal reveals that shalom is the connection between the parts that unify everything (*Netivot Olam, Netiv HaShalom* 1). When a person lives in peace with others, everything is whole. Since shalom effects completeness, every blessing in the *siddur* (prayer book) concludes with shalom. The creation of the world was completed on Shabbat, which is associated with shalom. For this reason, we light the candles for the sake of *shalom bayit* at the onset of Shabbat (*Mishnah Berurah* 263:30).

Shalom – The Unification of Opposites

The Hebrew word shalom is not identical with its English translation "peace," which refers to the absence of war and tumult. When people say, "Leave me in peace!" they mean, "Leave me alone, don't disturb me. Let me have my own peace and quiet!" The meaning of this kind of "peace" is division like its homonym "piece." On the other hand, the Hebrew term shalom means completion and does not refer to the absence of conflict but rather to the ultimate unification of opposites. The main purpose of creation is shalom. For this reason, the heavens (*shamayim*) that were created first encompass this unification. They consist of the opposite elements of *esh* (fire) and *mayim* (water). The only way they can be connected is through shalom. This is the meaning of "…He makes shalom above" (*Iyov 25:2*).

Unification of Male and Female is Beyond Nature

Unlike "peace" which is best achieved when a person is alone, the unification of man and woman in the bond of marriage involves merging the opposite male and female energies. Although one aspect of shalom is when each person stands in his own sphere without entering the boundary of his fellow, the *shalom bayit* of the Jewish home corresponds to the way Hashem unifies the heavens consisting of the opposing elements of fire and water. This unification does not conform to the ways of nature. The achievement of shalom lifts us above our existence in the physical world and connects us with the spiritual realm.

Shechinah Between Them

When we walk in the way of Torah and justice, every step on our individual path is connected with the universal truth of the Torah. Each of our individualities merges to form a whole, wherein we still recognize the boundaries between our own sphere and that of the other. When there is shalom between man and woman, they are able to lift themselves up above their mere physical existence while drawing down the *Shechinah* from the upper world to unite with the lower world. This unification is the middle world of shalom which stands between [and effects the boundary of] the upper world and the lower world. In this way, the union of marriage becomes a unification of upper and lower worlds as Rabbi Akiva teaches, "When man and woman come together in holiness the *Shechinah* is between them" (*Sotah* 17a).

Parashat Ki Tetze

The mitzvah of sending away the mother bird before taking her eggs or fledglings teaches us a deep lesson about the greatness of motherhood. Ibn Ezra explains that the mother is essential; therefore she must be left alone and respected by the hunter. "If a bird's nest chance to be before you in the way in any tree, or on the earth, whether they be young ones or eggs, and the mother is crouching upon the young or upon the eggs, you shall not take the mother with the young. But you shall surely let the mother go, and take the young to you, that it may be well with you, and that you may prolong your days" (*Devarim* 22:6–7).

Respecting the Mother of Life

According to Ramban, the reward for sending away the mother bird is particularly great because this mitzvah entails such a deep and elevated matter. *Kli Yakar* notices that its reward is identical with the reward for keeping the commandment to honor our parents. Both *mitzvot* teach us that no being comes into the world without a mother giving birth. This chain of motherhood leads us back to Hashem – the original Mother, Who gave birth to the world. Had the world been eternal, without a Creator, there would be no reason to respect our parents. However, we believe that the first Mother shared her honor with all mothers emanating from her. Therefore, we must honor our parents, and also send away the mother bird. Since both of these *mitzvot* strengthen our belief in the creation of the world, their reward is to live a long life in this world. This is the foundation of *emunah*, as it states: "...the righteous person **lives** by his faith" (*Chavakuk* 2:4). By means of *emunah*, we cleave to the source of life and therefore, the reward for this is to live a long life.

For the Sake of Fixing the World

The mitzvah of sending away the mother bird is immediately followed by the reference to building a new house. Our sages explain this juxtaposition as follows: If you fulfill the mitzvah of sending away the mother bird, you will merit building a new home, since this mitzvah leads you to believe that G-d created and built the world (see Rashi, *Devarim* 22:8). Rabbi Eliyahu Kitov asks why the Torah forbids taking the mother bird from upon her young ones in the nest, when in general, it permits taking the life of any bird in order to serve the needs of humanity. Moreover, why did the Torah have mercy only on the mother, and not on the young ones? He explains that the little ones, as well as the eggs, belong to mankind, because G-d made us rulers over all animals. However, by what means do human beings merit to rule over the mother who is hovering over her fledglings? Her instinct to protect her little ones prevents her from flying away. For the sake of her baby birds, she is willing to risk being caught by the hunter. It is not befitting to cruelly take advantage of this noble character trait, which G-d imprinted in His creatures. Since this mother bird is involved in raising her offspring, which is the most essential way of *tikun haolam*, we must send her free. She may then go and build another nest, thereby fulfilling the will of her Creator by continuing to be involved in fixing the world. Although humankind is the ruler of all creation, we cannot subdue the spirit of G-d which He imparted to all of His creatures. The motherly instinct to protect her young is considered to be the manifestation of the spirit of G-d which keeps the world going.

Our Soul is a Mother Bird Released

Ramban brings a kabbalistic reason for the mitzvah of sending away the mother bird. He quotes Rabbi Rechmai from *Sefer HaBahir* who notes that the Torah emphasizes the mother more than the father. This is because the mother refers to the attribute of *binah*, often referred to as "intuition," as it states: "For the mother is called *binah*" (*Mishlei* 2:3). Like the mother who has the power to give birth, the attribute of *binah* gives birth to the seven lower *sefirot* (Divine emanations) embodied in the seven days of creation. These days teach us to have faith in G-d and His Divine providence. While we must release the mother bird which also alludes to the soul, and let her reunite with her Maker, she bequeaths us with her offspring; the teachings of faith and the good deeds that we acquire in this world are the children of our soul.

Parashat Ki Tavo

This Torah portion describes the blessings and the curses. The Jewish people are warned that terrible curses will overtake them, as a consequence of not listening to the voice of G-d and refusing to keep His *mitzvot*. One of the worst curses is the threat of a famine so horrible that even the most caring person is forced to behave in an extremely cruel manner. "The man that is tender among you, and most delicate, his eye shall be evil towards his brother and towards the wife of his bosom, and towards the remnant of his children whom he shall leave" (*Devarim* 28:54).

The Sensitive Man and Woman

The Torah describes the sensitive man and woman at length, each one by a separate verse. "The tender and delicate woman among you, who would not adventure to set the sole of her foot upon the ground for delicateness and tenderness, her eye shall be evil towards the husband of her bosom, and towards her son, and towards her daughter" (*Devarim* 28:56). Let us compare the verses that describe the tender among men and women. What is the difference between them? *Kli Yakar* notes that men are not naturally as delicate as women. Therefore, it was necessary to add the word "most" to the word "delicate" in reference to the man, to emphasize that even the most delicate man would act in this cruel way. However, among women one does not have to be especially delicate to be disgusted with the thought of acting in such a cruel fashion.

The verse describing the tender woman contains an additional phrase not paralleled in the description of the delicate man, since a man would never be portrayed in this manner. The phrase, "who would not adventure to set the sole of her foot upon the ground for delicateness and tenderness," teaches us about the pitfalls of taking femininity to its extreme and becoming excessively delicate.

Taking Responsibility

What does it mean to be too delicate to put "the sole of her foot upon the ground"? Perhaps it refers to someone who is overly passive and submissive? A person, who does not want to walk by herself, is someone who is afraid to take responsibility for her own life. She literally expects the man to carry her off her feet and take care of her, while she surrenders her life in his hand. Her main desire is to be swept away by her Prince Charming on his white horse. Our mother Rivkah rectified this overly feminine tendency. She is known for her initiative and decisiveness (see our teaching on *Parashat Toldot* on page 21).

Being Grounded

The expression "not to place the feet on the ground" can also refer to someone who is not grounded – a dreamer disconnected with the bleak reality. There are women who stay aloof in their ivory tower; reading novels and gazing at the sparkling stars, unwilling to get their feet dirty in the murky mud of daily chores. Rabbi Akiva's wife, Rachel, was able to connect her lofty visionary dream with the tough reality of simple living. In order to transform a plain sheepherder into a Torah scholar of the highest caliber; she willingly descended from the ivory castle of her youth (see *Ketuvot* 62b–63a).

Taking a Stand

Finally, "not placing her feet on the ground" is associated with being afraid to take a stand. Our Mother Sarah teaches us to stand up for our beliefs. She did not let anything sway her from the resolve to safeguard the future of her son, Yitzchak, by demanding that Yishmael be expelled from her home (*Bereishit* 21:10). She was certainly not afraid to "put her foot down," and take a stand. As women, we must be careful to develop our will and assertiveness. We must choose a direction and stand up for truth even if we have to go against the grain.

Parashat Nitzavim

"You stand positioned this day all of you before Hashem your G-d; your heads of your tribes, your elders, and your officers, with all the people of Israel; your little ones, your wives, and your stranger that is in your camp..." (*Devarim* 29:9–10).

Depending on Their Mothers

Rabbi S.R. Hirsch notes that it states, "your wives," without the binding word "and." This implies that the wives are not placed next to their children, but rather the children and the wives are considered as one. G-d only relies on the children as long as He can trust their mothers. The spiritual and ethical future of the children is dependent on how dedicated the women are to G-d.

Separated in Holiness

According to Malbim, the Torah mentioned "your wives" separately, in order to highlight that they were standing by themselves and not mixed together with their husbands. At this holy moment when Israel entered the covenant with G-d, everyone was positioned in his or her own particular place. This was not a time for a family picnic. Male and female energy was clearly separated. Why is this segregation so central to Judaism? Why can I not sit at my husband's side in the place of prayer? Men and women do not have to separate during all our mundane chores. The Torah does not require separate men's and women's hours in the department store, so why can we not remain together during the holiest moments?

In Their Own Separate Position

Prior to receiving the Torah, Israel was commanded to abstain from intimate relations for three days (*Shemot* 19:15). Now again, when confirming the covenant of the Torah, division was necessary. The true connection between male and female energies is, by its very nature, sexual. This union, when performed in purity and holiness, becomes the channel for the Divine Presence, and for conceiving holy souls. However, there are other kinds of associations between male and female energy that distract from communion with G-d. On an energetic level, men and women relate differently to Hashem. We do not sing in the same key, nor do we dance to the same beat. Powerful male energy can crush a woman and make her forget herself and her place with G-d. Likewise, powerful female energy, when recklessly exposed to any man, may distract his focus on G-d. On the other hand, when a woman stands alone or side by side with another woman, it helps her connect with her spirit and express her own inner space which she yearns to fill and devote to Hashem.

A Direct Connection

G-d's mercy extends to all His creatures equally, both male and female. "Although Hashem has appointed for us heads, elders, and bailiffs, we are all equal before Him as it states: 'with all the people of Israel…'" (*Midrash Tanchuma, Nitzavim* 2). Even if women have a more passive role in the synagogue, we do not receive our spirituality indirectly through the men. Contrary to other religions, neither the rabbis nor the husbands become intermediaries that enable women to relate to G-d. Women are mentioned separately when standing before G-d, to teach that we all have the opportunity to turn to G-d on our own. Channah, the Mother of our Prayer, stood alone before G-d when she poured out her soul. Even without the male prayer rituals such as a *minyan* (prayer quorum), *tefillin*, (phylacteries) and *talit* (prayer shawl), she was able to teach both men and women a new level of prayer. The text of our central prayer, the *amidah*, is modeled after her heartfelt supplication (*Berachot* 31a).

We Come to G-d Alone

Being in communion with G-d is a very intimate practice. Our inner essence is revealed as we stand before Him, pouring out our hearts. When a woman stands before G-d, she must be alone in order to be completely open and devoted to the Divine. No other bond can block or stand in the way of becoming one with G-d. Inside that very deep place within us that we share with our soul mate, there must always remain a point dedicated to no one but G-d. We come to G-d alone, with only the naked essence of our being, distinct from all other individuals. Before G-d, this essence can never dissolve and become lost in the identity of another.

Parashat Vayelech

Parashat Vayelech includes the mitzvah of *hakhel* requiring all the Jewish people to gather together in the place Hashem had chosen, (*Yerushalayim*), at the end of every seven-year *shemittah* cycle. "Gather (*hakhel*) the people together, men, and women, and children, and your convert that is within your gate that they may hear..." (*Devarim* 31:12).

The Mitzvah of Hakhel

Rambam describes the mitzvah of *hakhel* as follows: During the night following the first holiday of Sukkot, all the men, women, children and converts would assemble at the women's courtyard of the Temple. They would hear select parts of the Torah from the book of *Devarim* read aloud by the king. These parts included the two first paragraphs of the *Shema Yisrael* prayer as well as the blessings and the curses in *Parashat Ki Tavo* (*Mishneh Torah*, The Laws of Holidays, Chapter 3). According to *Sefer HaChinuch,* since Torah is our essence, praise and splendor, it is fitting that men, women and children should gather together at specific times in order to hear her words. The experience of this great gathering would reverberate through the entire people, filling their hearts with desire for the Torah and making them learn to know G-d as it states: "...that they may learn, and fear Hashem your G-d, and observe to do all the words of this Torah" (*Devarim* 31:12).

Bringing the Lessons of Shemittah Home

According to Rabbi Menachem Mendel Schneerson of Lubavitch, *hakhel* takes place at the end of the *shemittah* cycle in order that the lessons learned from keeping the laws of *shemittah* should spill over into the coming years. The selected Torah paragraphs read during *hakhel* help inculcate into our very nature the main lesson of *shemittah*: that G-d is in charge of the world. When we understand that everything that we possess belongs to G-d, we can accept the Torah covenant, including the sections describing the blessings and the curses.

What is the connection between *shemittah* and the holiday of Sukkot? The laws of *shemittah* decrease the gap between the rich and the poor, since no one has ownership over the produce of his field, and all monetary debts are released. This causes brotherhood and peace among Israel, as does dwelling in our temporary booths during Sukkot. Unity opens the hearts of Israel to absorb the lessons of the Torah. Therefore, all of Israel unifies on Sukkot, following the *shemittah* year, to hear the king read aloud selected sections from the Torah (*Kli Yakar, Devarim* 31:12).

Unity, Love, and Equality

Rabbeinu Bachaya explains that although people have different levels of intelligence and comprehension, each segment of society practices the laws that apply individually to them. The Torah addresses us all equally, including the child, the youth, and the advanced in years, the wise, and the foolish. As Scripture states, "…you shall read this Torah before **all Israel** in their ears" (*Devarim* 31:11). Only afterwards does it state, "Gather the people together…" (*Devarim* 31:12). *Me'or v'Shemesh* notes that the order of the mitzvah of *hakhel* is unusual. Gathering all Israel together is mentioned only after reading the Torah to them. Doesn't one need to first gather everyone together in order to read the Torah to the entire people? The reversed order alludes to the final goal of *hakhel*, which is to engender unity among the Jewish people. The lesson that must be read "in their ears," is to gather together as one person and love one another from small to great, including those who are "going off the *derech*" (leaving the Torah path). This greater unity among "men, women, children and converts" will enable us all to listen, learn, and see Hashem.

Women Are Not Exempt from the Torah

Rambam and *Sefer HaChinuch* conclude that the general principle that women are exempt from the time bound positive *mitzvot* does not pertain to all cases. We learn this from the mitzvah of *hakhel*, in which the women are included, as it states: "Gather the people together, men, **women** and children..." (*Devarim* 31:12). The fact that women are obligated to hear the Torah being read during *hakhel*, indicates that they are included in the mitzvah of learning Torah. As early as the twelfth century, Rabbi Yehudah HaChassid wrote in *Sefer Chassidim* 313 that a person is obligated to teach his daughters to fulfill Torah laws. Otherwise, how can they be expected, for example, to keep Shabbat if they do not know the laws of Shabbat? In the days of King Chezkiyahu, both men and women knew all the laws of purity and sacrifices. The Shunamite woman likewise would go to hear Elisha teach every *Rosh Chodesh* and Shabbat (2 *Melachim* 4:23).

Men to Learn and Women to Listen

"That they may hear, and that they may learn." The Talmud concludes, "The men come to learn while the women come to listen" (*Chagigah* 3a). It seems discriminatory that women are only permitted to audit. Are women not considered capable of learning Torah properly, in the manner expected of men? Perhaps we are underestimating the importance of being a good listener. Actually, the mitzvah of *hakhel* was geared towards teaching the entire people to develop good listening skills as it states: "...to read this Torah before all Israel in their ears" (*Devarim* 31:11). The word *shema* (listen) appears fifty-two times in the selected *hakhel* Torah readings, which includes the first two paragraphs of the *Shema* Prayer.

Integral listening has become a new concept in modern psychology. Listening is hard work, explains Diane Bone in *The Business of Listening*. Active listening is more than just a skill; it's also a matter of attitude. In order to hear the message, we must be present, pay proper attention, look at the speaker and stop other tasks, not allowing interruptions to distract us. We must select the information that is most important and recognize emotional messages before forming an opinion. When words, issues, situations and personalities trigger our "hot buttons," we tend to distort the message we are hearing and tune out or prejudge the message and/or the speaker. Being an active listener, involves the whole body. Not only the ears need to be tuned in, but also the eyes, intellect, and the entire being. Developing good listening skills is one of the main objectives of the mitzvah of *hakhel* as its selected reading implores us: "Hear O Yisrael, Hashem our G-d, Hashem is One" (*Devarim* 6:4). Since women are praised for the ability to listen, perhaps this is why the mitzvah of *hakhel* took place in the women's courtyard of the Temple.

Reward for Bringing the Children

"...That their children, who have not known anything, may hear, and learn to fear Hashem your G-d..." (*Devarim* 31:13). I wonder how it would be possible to hear even one word of the Torah, without being interrupted by the crying, cooing, fighting, and laughing of all the children who were present during *hakhel.*

The Talmud explains that the children were brought in order to reward those who bring them (*Chagigah* 3a). The mothers certainly deserved reward for their wisdom of ensuring their children's impeccable behavior. The *Shelah*, however, warns us not to learn from the mitzvah of *hakhel* to bring children unsupervised to the synagogue where they are apt to disturb the service (*Mesechet Tamid* 54:76). "To reward those who bring them" may also refer to the fact that educating our children in Torah, actually gives us the opportunity to raise ourselves up as well. When Yehudah, son of Leah, realized that he was going downhill in a spiritual crisis, he became busy taking a wife, in order to bear children to educate in Torah and thereby elevate himself. (*Arugat HaBosem, Parashat Vayeishev*). We are privileged to be able to raise children and ensure that they be surrounded by Torah. It takes great wisdom and foresight to be organized in a way that allows us to bring our infants to Torah *shiurim* (classes) without disrupting the learning. By exposing our children to the words of our holy Torah, we not only gather inspiration and knowledge, we glean eternal reward and elevation.

Parashat Ha'azinu

All the souls of Israel are contained in the Song of *Ha'azinu*, which reveals the Divine plan from beginning to end, including the purpose and *tikun* (rectification) of creation. According to Rashi, the statement "...you shall write for yourselves this whole song..." (*Devarim* 31:19), refers to the Song of *Ha'azinu*, whereas the Talmud derives the positive mitzvah to write a Torah scroll from this same verse (*Sanhedrin* 21b).

Full Circle

Our sages teach that the Song of *Ha'azinu* is great because it contains the present, past, and future. It includes both this world and the coming world. The Hebrew translation of the word "song," *shir*, is connected to the word *sharsheret*, which means chain. The word *shir* is linked to the concept of "coming full circle." All songs within the Torah are associated with the completion of an episode, when all its details are woven together to form complete harmony. For this reason, Moshe, the head of all prophets, could only recite this song when his entire life was behind him.

The Inwardly Receptive Mother Earth

According to *Chizkuni*, Moshe prayed that his words of Torah would bring forth beautiful fruits in the hearts of those who heard them, just like the rain and the dew makes everything grow: "Give ear (*ha'azinu*),

O you heavens, and I will speak; and hear (*tishma*), O earth, the words of my mouth. My doctrine shall drop as the rain; my speech shall flow as the dew…" (*Devarim* 32:1–2). The heavens are a metaphor for the masculine, while the earth alludes to the feminine; hence the term "Mother Earth." The heavens bestow rain upon earth which, like the mother's womb, nurtures and brings forth its Divine fruits

> *Kabbalah, as the science of the relationship between G-d and humankind, employs, as its primary metaphor, the interplay of masculine and feminine energies…to describe the deepest mysteries of creation, the unfolding of worlds…Kabbalah bases its use of the terms masculine and feminine on the physical differences between males and females. The active bestower and outward extending principle is called masculine, while the inward, receptive, and form building principle is called feminine* (Sarah Yehudit Schneider, *Prayer and Destiny*).

The Feminine Caress of Dew – A Delight for All

Why mention both rain and dew? Rain, which falls from the heavens, is a potent and forceful masculine phenomenon. Dew, on the other hand, appears imperceptibly, softly caressing and nourishing every little herb. We all notice when rain drops down from heaven. However, only by recognizing the moisture of the earth, do we realize that dew came from above. While the masculine power is easily noticed, its feminine counterpart is only uncovered through careful scrutiny of its gentle effect upon the world. Although we only need the masculine rain at certain times, since an excessive downpour can be harmful, we can never get too much of feminine dew. As Rashi explains, the reason the Torah added the word "dew" is that rain sometimes annoys people, for instance those on a journey, whereas everybody rejoices in the dew.

In Tune With the Divine Will

Ohr HaChayim notes that the verb connected with "heaven" is written in the active voice (*ha'azinu*), whereas the verb linked to "earth" is in the passive form (*tishma*). Perhaps this alludes to the reality that men are obligated to give ear and listen very carefully to the precepts of the Torah, while women are naturally attuned to its insights. This is why the Torah did not need to command the earth to give ear, for it is bound to listen of its own accord. Sensitivity to hear the deeper message beyond words is a feminine quality that we all need to enhance. The gift of *binah yeterah* (additional intuition) attributed to women helps us perceive the needs of others, and fathom the will of G-d. As we open ourselves to receive G-d's eternal message, we become like Mother Earth, molding and bringing into fruition all the latent goodness of life.

Parashat Vezot Haberachah

Moshe's blessing to Israel before his passing away includes the following prelude: "Moshe commanded us Torah, the inheritance (*morasha*) of the congregation of Ya'acov" (*Devarim* 33:4). Rashi reads the verse as follows: "The Torah that Moshe commanded us is an inheritance for the congregation of Ya'acov. We have taken it and will never abandon it." This implies that the Torah of Moshe has become ingrained within the entire Jewish people to the extent that we are unable to ever separate ourselves from it.

The Crown of Torah is Free for All

The *Sifri* explains that every Jew has a share in the Torah, as it states: "You stand this day **all of you** before Hashem your G-d..." (*Devarim* 29:9). This idea is reflected in the saying of our sages that there exist three crowns: The crown of Torah, the crown of *Kehuna* (priesthood), and the crown of Kingdom. The crown of *Kehuna* was given to the children of Aharon and the crown of Kingdom to the offspring of David. However, the crown of Torah is available to whoever wants to take it (*Kohelet Rabbah* 7:2).

Women May Receive the Crown of Torah

Although a woman can neither aspire to become a king from the Davidic dynasty nor a *Kohen*, the crown of the Torah is available to her. During all generations of Jewish history, there have always been great and learned women. There were renowned women such as Devorah, the wife of Lapidot, for whom hordes of people would wait in line to pose halachic inquiries. Beruriah of the Talmud, taught her husband how to have mercy on others, and Rashi's daughters participated in the *pilpul* (dialectics) of their scholarly husbands. These are just examples, yet there were many less well-known female scholars throughout the generations, who taught men behind a *mechitzah* (partition). In our own time, we are privileged to learn from outstanding *talmidot chachamot* (learned women) specializing both in the revealed and hidden Torah. There is a renewed thirst among observant Jewish women to delve in depth into the classical texts of the Torah and its commentaries. Everywhere, new *midrashot* for women are sprouting forth, packed with spiritual Jewish women seeking to return not only to their roots, but also to serious textual Torah study. No longer do lectures satisfy their yearning. The new generation of women wants more than just to sit back passively and listen to the wisdom of others. They are ready to work hard, together with their study partners, in order to gain the necessary skills to enable them to struggle through Torah texts with the assistance of their rabbis and mentors.

Queen of the Living Torah

The verse, "Hear my son the reproach of your father and do not forsake the Torah of your mother" (*Mishlei* 1:8), is gaining new meaning in our time. Just as a mother gives life to others, so does she ignite the light of Torah in her children, her soul sisters, and herself. Our desire for learning is much more than an intellectual pursuit. We want to learn in order to live a life of Torah, infusing the whole world with its spirit. Women from all walks of life are struggling with learning Hebrew vowels, saying *brachot*, understanding halachic terminology, separating *challah* and wearing skirts. We are eating in the Sukkah, praying and meditating in the fields, picking luscious purple grapes in the Land of Israel and taking tithes. Our learning and living merge to become one, as we endeavor to bring the *geulah* one step closer.

Women's Learning Returns the Shechinah

According to the Midrash, the Torah is engaged to the Jewish people, like a bride to her groom. This is learned from the following pun: "Do not read '*morasha*,' a possession, but rather '*meurasa*' engaged, for the Torah is engaged to Israel" (*Yalkut Shimoni*, *Devarim* 33:951). Rabbeinu Bachaya explains that according to Kabbalah, the Torah is called Rachel, who is engaged to Ya'acov. From the time that the *Shechinah* departed, "Rachel is weeping for her children" until the return of the *Shechinah* during the redemption when Rachel once again becomes Ya'acov's wife. This is the meaning of "...they shall come back again from the land of the enemy" (*Yirmeyahu* 31:15). The fact that the Torah is called Rachel testifies that her essence is, indeed, female. One of the manifestations of exile has been a lack of feminine viewpoints on the Torah. Today, we are fortunate to experience the return of the Feminine Indwelling Presence, embodied by the revival of authentic learning and living the Torah of the Mothers by the daughters of Israel.

Biographies of Commentators

Medieval Torah Commentators

אונקלוס Onkelos, (circa 35–120), from Israel is identified as the convert Aquila of Sinope, a student of Rabbi Akiva and possible a kinsman of the Roman emperor, Hadrian, at the time of the *Tana'im* (the scholars of the Mishnah during the Roman period, after the destruction of the Second Temple in the first century.) He is the author of the renowned *Targum Onkelos*, the official translation of the Torah to Aramaic. From Talmudic times, and to this day in Yemenite Jewish communities, *Targum Onkelos* is recited by heart as a verse-by-verse translation alternately with the Hebrew verses of the Torah in the synagogue. The Talmud states, "A person should complete the weekly Torah portion along with the community, reading it twice with the *Targum* once" (*Berachot* 8b). This passage is universally accepted to refer to *Targum Onkelos*, whose explanations carry authoritative weight and are quoted by Rashi frequently. Referenced on pages 15, 36.

רש"י Rashi, Rabbi Shlomo ben Yitzchak, (1040–1105), from Troyes, France was a leading commentator on the Torah and the Talmud, a grammarian, and legal authority. Having studied in Worms and Mainz, his commentaries are distinguished by great clarity, and concise language. More than two hundred super-commentaries are written on Rashi's work, which was the first Hebrew book published (1475). His commentaries on both the Torah and the Talmud are still the main studied commentaries today, as they are considered the most inclusive and authoritative in Jewish scholarship. Rashi inherited a vineyard and supported his family through viticulture. Referenced on almost every page.

רשב"ם Rashbam, Rabbi Shmuel ben Meir, (1083–1174), from Ramerupt, France was the son of Meir ben Shemuel and the grandson of Rashi. He studied with both of them. It is clear from Rashbam's commentaries that some of them were written, or at least developed in Rashi's presence. On some occasions Rashi accepted Rashbam's opinions and amended his commentary accordingly. Rashbam was a talmudist and teacher of his illustrious brother, Rabbeinu Tam. He raised sheep and wine grapes like his grandfather, Rashi. Referenced on page 132.

דעת זקנים מבעלי התוספות *Da'at Zekeinim M'ba'alei HaTosfot – Masters of the Additions*, (12th–13th centuries, Ashkenazi), from Germany and France. The Tosafists were collectively the authors of the commentary known as the *Tosfot*, which appears in most Talmud editions side by side with Rashi's commentary on nearly every page. Their commentary on the Torah is included in *Mikra'ot Gedolot* (the standard Hebrew Torah reader with selected commentaries) together with the most prominent and popular Torah commentaries. Referenced on pages 32, 36.

ריה"ל Rihal, Rabbi Yehudah HaLevi, (1086–1145), from Toledo, Spain was the greatest Hebrew poet of his time. His famous innovative philosophical work *The Kuzari* written as a dialogue between the *Khazar* King and the Rabbi foreshadowed religious Zionism. At the end of his life Rabbi Yehudah HaLevi immigrated to Israel, but was tragically murdered by an Arab soon after he arrived in the Holy Land. He supported his family as a renowned physician. Referenced on page 76.

ראב"ע Rabbi Avraham Ibn Ezra, (1089–1164), from Tudela, Spain was one of the most distinguished Jewish scholars and writers of the middle ages. Ibn Ezra excelled in philosophy, astronomy/astrology, medicine, poetry, linguistics/grammar and Biblical exegesis; he was called "The wise, great and admirable doctor." Ibn Ezra's main work is his commentary on the Torah, which has a number of super-commentaries. He was very poor and lived his life as a wandering scholar crossing continents and passing through numerous countries from Europe to North Africa where he met the Rambam. He even visited the Land of Israel. Referenced on pages 47, 66, 89, 133, 176.

רמב"ם Rambam, Rabbi Moshe ben Maimon – Maimonides, (1135–1204), from Spain, Morocco, and Egypt was the most influential Jewish thinker of the middle ages. He was the first to write a systematic code of Halachah, the *Mishneh Torah*, which became the model for the *Shulchan Aruch*, (the sixteenth century code of Jewish law). He also wrote the philosophical work, *The Guide to the Perplexed*. Rambam, known as a rationalist, excelled in the fields of logic, science, exegesis and medicine. He served as physician to the sultan of Egypt, wrote numerous books on medicine, and in his "spare time" served as leader of Cairo's Jewish Community. Rambam was one of the medieval Jewish philosophers who also influenced the non-Jewish world. Although his works on Jewish law and ethics were initially met with opposition during his lifetime, he became acknowledged as one of the foremost rabbinical authorities and philosophers in Jewish history. Today, his teachings are considered a cornerstone of Jewish thought and study. Referenced on pages 65, 67, 104, 106, 164, 170, 185, 187.

רבי יהודה החסיד Rabbi Yehudah HaChassid, (1150–1217), from Germany was leader of the German Pietists, who authored the religious guide, *Sefer Chassidim* (The Book of the Pious). This unique and engaging halachic and ethical work contains a highly valuable account of the day-to-day religious life of medieval German Jews known as *Chassidim* (Pious Ones) and addresses their concern. Though the work is nonsystematic, it presents the combined teachings of the three leaders of German *Chassidim* during the twelfth and thirteenth centuries, Shemuel the *Chassid*, Yehudah the *Chassid* of Regensburg (his son), and Elazar ben Yehudah of Worms. Referenced on page 187.

רד"ק **Radak, Rabbi David Kimchi**, (1160–1235), from Narbonne, France was a Torah commentator, grammarian and philosopher. Radak composed a dictionary of the Hebrew language. He is best known today for his commentaries on the books of the Prophets that focus on the language, grammar, and literal meaning of the words, while sometimes addressing historical and geographical questions. However, his commentary on *Bereishit* is philosophical, ethical and mystical. Radak was influenced by both Ibn Ezra and the Rambam, who he staunchly defended in the debates over his writings. Referenced on page 115.

רמב"ן **Ramban, Rabbi Moshe ben Nachman** – Nachmanides, (1194–1270), from Catalonia, Spain was the foremost halachist of his age and one of the leading authors of talmudic literature. His commentary on the Torah is the first to incorporate the teachings of Kabbalah. In addition to his commentary on Torah and Halachah, he wrote more than fifty lucid and logical works. Ramban was an outspoken Zionist and declared it a mitzvah to take possession of Israel and to live there. (Ramban, *Bemidbar* 33:53). Ramban was a skilled physician and poet. At age 72, he resettled in the Land of Israel. Referenced on pages 28, 41, 55, 56, 67, 79, 99, 100, 101, 106, 107, 155, 176, 177.

חיזקוני ***Chizkuni*, Rabbi Chezekiah ben Manoach**, (13th century), from France wrote a kabbalistic commentary on the *Chumash* (Pentateuch), under the title *Chizkuni*. He quotes certain *Midrashim* which appear nowhere else, and like Rashi, he translates obscure Hebrew words into French. *Chizkuni* was not printed until 1524 in Venice, Italy. It is mainly based on Rashi, but also uses about twenty other commentaries, though the author quotes as his sources only Rashi, Dunash ben Labrat, the Yossippon, and the Physica. Referenced on pages 31, 36, 190.

ספר החינוך ***Sefer HaChinuch*, The Book of Education**, was published anonymously in thirteenth century Spain. Some scholars ascribe its authorship to Rabbi Aharon HaLevi of Barcelona (circa 1235–1290), a talmudic scholar and halachist. Others disagree, as the views of *Sefer HaChinuch* contradict opinions held by HaLevi in other works. This has led to the conclusion that the true author to *Sefer HaChinuch* was a different Rabbi Aharon HaLevi, a student of the Rashba, rather than his colleague. *Sefer HaChinuch* systematically discusses each of the six hundred thirteen *mitzvot* separately, both from a legal and a moral perspective. Based upon Rambam's system of counting in his *Sefer HaMitzvot*, *Sefer HaChinuch* links each mitzvah to its source in the Torah, according to its order in the weekly Torah portion. Afterwards it addresses its philosophical root (*shoresh*). It presents a brief overview of the Halachah governing its observance and closes with a summary about the mitzvah's applicability. Referenced on pages 107, 169, 173, 185, 187.

רבנו בחיי Rabbeinu Bachaya, Rabbi Bachaya ben Asher, (circa 1250–1340), was from Saragossa, Spain where he served as a *dayan* (Torah judge). His commentary to the Torah, noted for introducing Kabbalah into the study of Torah, received such popularity that it has been reprinted twenty-three times and has more than ten super-commentaries. In his profound kabbalistic insights he often quotes Ramban and the *Zohar*. Referenced on pages 5, 19, 28, 35, 59, 63, 79, 105, 165, 172, 173, 186, 195.

בעל הטורים *Ba'al HaTurim*, Rabbi Ya'acov ben Asher, (1269–1343), from Cologne, Germany was an influential medieval rabbinic authority and the author of *Arba'ah Turim*, one of the most important halachic books of all times. Rabbi Ya'acov moved to Toledo, Spain with his father and lived in poverty most of his life. His tersely written commentary on the Torah which can be found in the *Mikra'ot Gedolot*, gleans hidden messages based on *gematria* (drawing associations between words whose numerical values are equivalent), acrostics, formations of letters, and Scriptural word patterns. Referenced on pages 99, 157.

רלב"ג Ralbag, Rabbi Levi ben Gershom, (1288–1344), from Bagnols sur-Cèze, France was a mathematician, astronomer, philosopher, and Torah commentator. He had very broad intellectual interests and contributed to many areas of human studies including scientific, talmudic, liturgical and philosophical learning. An eminent talmudist, Ralbag was also consulted on questions of Halachah. In his voluminous Torah commentary, he discusses diverse questions of philosophical and ethical nature such as the problem of providence, miracles, and Mashiach. Referenced on page 65.

אברבנאל Abarbanel, Rabbi Yitzchak ben Yehudah, (1437–1508), from Lisbon, Portugal was a Jewish statesman, philosopher, Torah commentator, and financier. He was born into a family descended from King David, distinguished by financial, political and Jewish communal leadership achievements. His family had strong moral convictions, and loved scholarship, and piety. His commentary on the Torah is characterized by its long list of detailed questions which are answered systematically in logical almost scientific style. Referenced on pages 10, 27, 31, 47.

ספורנו *Sforno*, Rabbi Ovadiah ben Ya'acov, (circa 1470–1550), from Cesena, Italy was a Torah commentator, halachist, master of Hebrew, philosopher and physician. Rabbi Ovadiah focused on the literal meaning (*peshat*) of the text, avoiding mystical and kabbalistic interpretations, while emphasizing the inner connection between different parts of a verse and explaining duplications in phraseology. His commentary contains frequent references to humanistic ideas, inculcating love not only for fellow Jews, but for the righteous gentile and mankind in general. Referenced on pages 13, 31, 32, 137.

רב אליהו מזרחי The Re'em, Rabbi Eliyahu Mizrachi, (circa 1455–1526), from Constantinople where he served as the Chief Rabbi, was a talmudist and halachic authority (*posek*). He is best known for his *Sefer HaMizrachi*, one of the most important super-commentaries on Rashi's commentary on the Torah. It is counted in its own right among the most important Torah commentaries. The work was first published in Venice in 1527 after Rabbi Mizrachi's death. It cites Rashi's talmudic and midrashic sources, and elucidates all obscure passages. *Sefer HaMizrachi* was written, partially, to defend Rashi from the strictures of the later commentators, particularly the Ramban. Referenced on page 147.

כלי יקר ***Kli Yakar*, Rabbi Ephraim Solomon ben Aaron of Luntshits**, (1550–1619), from Leczyca, Poland was a renowned preacher who served as president of the rabbinical court in Prague and *Rosh Yeshiva* in Lemberg. He was distinguished for his lucid and fascinating sermons which were collected and published in various books. His commentary on the Torah, *Kli Yakar* (Lublin, 1602), is included in *Mikra'ot Gedolot* together with the most prominent and popular Torah commentaries. Referenced on pages 4, 11, 14, 16, 20, 43, 48, 59, 111, 176, 179, 186.

מהרש"א ***Maharsha*, Rabbi Shemuel Eidels**, (1555–1631), from Krakow, Poland was famous for his commentary on the Talmud, *Chiddushei Halachot*, a keenly analytical commentary on the Talmud, with a focus on *Tosfot*. It is said that if one grasps the *Maharsha*, then one has understood the *Tosfot*. This commentary was quickly accepted and printed in almost all editions of the Talmud. The *Maharsha* established a yeshiva in Posen, served as rabbi in Chelm, Lublin, and Ostrog and was active in the Council of the Four Lands. He also wrote an extensive commentary on the aggadic (non legalistic parts) of the Talmud, reflecting a wide knowledge of philosophy and Kabbalah. Referenced on pages 47, 48, 63.

Torah Mystics

זוהר ***Zohar – Radiance***, the most important work of Kabbalah, is a mystical commentary on the Torah compiled into several books. It discusses the nature of G-d, the origin and structure of the universe, the nature of souls, sin, redemption, good and evil, and the relationship between G-d and man. Most of the *Zohar* is written in the exalted style of Aramaic, spoken in the Land of Israel during the Roman period in the first two centuries. It first appeared in Spain in the thirteenth century, and was published by Moshe de Leon who ascribed this work to Rabbi Shimon bar Yochai, one of the foremost disciples of Rabbi Akiva from the period of the *Tana'im*. During the Roman persecution, Rabbi Shimon hid in a cave for thirteen years, studying Torah with his son, Elazar and receiving revelations from Eliyahu the Prophet which were recorded in the *Zohar*. Referenced on pages 37, 84, 135, 162.

מהר"ל Maharal, Rabbi Yehudah Loew ben Betzalel, (circa 1520–1609), from Prague was an important talmudic scholar, Jewish mystic and philosopher who served as the Chief Rabbi of Prague for most of his life. He wrote a book on every holiday, but is best known for his super-commentary, the *Gur Aryeh*, on Rashi's Torah commentary. *Chiddushei Aggadot*, his three volume commentary on the aggadic part of the Talmud, demonstrates how seemingly opposing opinions in the Talmud are different aspects of the greater whole. Kabbalistic ideas permeate Maharal's writings in a rational and philosophic tone. His main kabbalistic influences were the *Zohar* and *Sefer Yetzirah* as Lurianic Kabbalah (Ariza"l's teachings) had not yet reached Europe during his time. Maharal is the forerunner for Chassidism, especially its Polish branch. He also inspired modern Torah scholars such as Rabbi Avraham Yitzchak Kook and Rabbi Eliyahu Dessler. Referenced on pages 19, 20, 70, 130, 137, 139, 145, 173.

אריז"ל Ariza"l, Rabbi Yitzchak Luria Ashkenazi, (1534–1572), from Jerusalem was a leading kabbalist with a tremendous impact upon the Jewish world, particularly the world of Chassidism. He learned from the Radbaz, author of more than three thousand halachic responsa. Ariza"l was an expert in *Tanach* (Bible), Mishnah, Talmud, Midrash, and Kabbalah. He knew the mysteries of *gilgul* (reincarnation), could read faces in the manner outlined in the *Zohar*, and had the ability to discern everything an individual had done and would do in the future. At the young age of thirty-six, only two and a half years before his death, he settled in the city of Tzefat, known as the center of Kabbalah. There he became the leader of a small group of scholars who delved into the mysteries of the Torah. Lurianic Kabbalah can be described as a mystical interpretation of exile and redemption, through the process of *tikun* (rectification). Ariza"l revealed his secret teachings to Rabbi Chayim Vital who put them into writing. Referenced on pages xxxi, 14, 24, 77.

רב משה אלשיך Rabbi Moshe Alshech, (1508–1593), from Turkey emigrated to Israel, settling in Tzefat, where he became a student of Rabbi Yosef Karo. In Tzefat he gained prominence as a halachic authority and inspiring teacher. His commentaries on the Torah and the Prophets, supported by ample quotations from Talmud and Midrash, are based on his weekly *parashah* lectures delivered every Shabbat before large audiences. They became very popular and are still studied today, largely because of their powerful and practical teachings on leading a virtuous life. Although Alschech belonged to the circle of kabbalists from Tzefat, his works rarely betray traces of the Kabbalah. Alschech began each section with a number of questions, which he proceeded to answer. His objective was to glean a moral lesson from each word of Scripture to support concepts such as, trust in G-d, patient endurance, and the vanity of materialism as compared with the everlasting bliss of the World to Come. Referenced on page 68.

השל״ה הקדוש The *Shelah HaKadosh*, Rabbi Yesha'ya Horowitz, (1565–1630), from Prague was a well-known mystic who studied under the Maharam of Lublin. He was a wealthy and active philanthropist, supporting Torah learning especially in Jerusalem. After serving as rabbi in many European prominent cities and assuming the prestigious position of Rabbi of Prague, he immigrated to Israel in 1620 and settled in Tzefat. The *Shelah* stressed the joy in every action, and how to transform the evil inclination into good in his many kabbalistic, and halachic works. His most important work is *Shenei Luchoth HaBrit* (Two Tablets of the Covenant); abbreviated *Shelah* של״ה. The work is an encyclopedic compilation of ritual, ethics, and mysticism from both the Written and Oral Torah. It had a profound impact on Jewish life, and greatly influenced the Ba'al Shem Tov and the development of the Chassidic movement. Rabbi Shneur Zalman of Liadi was described as a "*Shelah Yid*," and the *Shelah* clearly echoes in the *Tanya*. Referenced on page 188.

אור החיים *Ohr HaChayim*, Rabbi Chayim ben Attar, (1696–1742), from Morocco was a Torah commentator, kabbalist, and talmudist. He briefly served as Rabbi in Italy before making *aliyah* (immigrating) to Israel, first settling in Acco, then moving to Jerusalem and starting a yeshiva there. He received his name, the *Ohr HaChayim*, from the most famous of his works, his classical commentary on the Torah, found in most editions of *Mikra'ot Gedolot*. In this work he uses all four methods of Torah interpretation: *peshat* – the simple meaning; *derash* – what is understood from between the lines; *remez* – allusion; and *sod* – the mystical kabbalistic level. Rabbi Chayim became famous for his Torah knowledge and saintliness at a young age. He declined payment for his services as rabbi, and preferred to earn his money as a very skilled goldsmith. On the day that Rabbi Chayim came to Jerusalem, the Ba'al Shem Tov told his students, "Today Mashiach ben Yosef entered Jerusalem." Referenced on pages 15, 16, 22, 28, 130, 191.

Chassidic Torah Commentators

רב יעקב יוסף Rabbi Ya'acov Yosef of Polnoye, (1710–1784), from Russia was one of the first and most dedicated disciples of the Ba'al Shem Tov, the founder of Chassidism. Ya'acov Yosef was already an accomplished scholar when he attached himself to the Ba'al Shem Tov. This engendered much controversy and caused him to be expelled from his position as the Rabbi of Shargorod. His book, *Toldot Ya'acov Yosef* (1780), was the first chassidic work ever published. It repeats the phrase, "I have heard from my teacher," two hundred forty-nine times. Referenced on page 69.

מאור ושמש *Me'or v'Shemesh*, Rabbi Kalonymus Kalman HaLevi Epstein, (circa 1753–1823), from Krakow, Poland was an *ilui* (young prodigy), who became known as an extraordinarily great and G-dly kabbalist, holy leader and miracle worker. Jews from far and wide came to hear his profound words of Torah and receive his guidance and blessings. He was the youngest and closest of all of Rabbi Elimelech of Lizhensk's students as well as his personal *shamash* (assistant). Rabbi Kalman arranged groups of *Chassidim* who prayed with *devekut* (ecstatic devotion) employing pronounced bodily movements. They were strongly opposed by the Krakow community; however, over time even Rabbi Kalman's fiercest opponents recognized his greatness and Rabbi Kalman succeeded in propagating Chassidism throughout western Galicia. His main work, *Me'or v'Shemesh*, a commentary on the Torah and the five *Megillot* (Scrolls) with allusions on the High Holidays was published in several editions. It is one of the fundamental works of Chassidism, and includes information on the activities and the personalities of *tzaddikim*. Referenced on page 186.

באר מים חיים ***Be'er Mayim Chayim*, Rabbi Chayim ben Solomon Tyrer of Czernowitz**, (circa 1760–1817), from Galicia, Poland was a chassidic leader, eloquent preacher and a talented writer. As a disciple of Yechiel Michael of Zloczow, Rabbi Chayim had a profound knowledge of rabbinical literature and mysticism. He later served as rabbi in Mogilev, Kishinev, Czernowitz district, and Botosani. Rabbi Chayim did much to spread Chassidism in Romania, and to prevent the *Haskalah* (the Enlightenment movement) from spreading. His resistance to certain government decrees forced him to relinquish his office in Czernowitz in 1807. In 1813 Rabbi Chayim immigrated to Israel and settled in Tzefat. He wrote the following works, which were published in many editions: *Siddur shel Shabbat*; *Be'er Mayim Chayim* (*Well of Living Waters*), a commentary on Torah, *Sha'ar ha-Tefillah*; and *Eretz HaChayim*. Referenced on pages 13, 29, 49.

רב צדוק מלובלין Rabbi Tzadok HaKohen of Lublin, (1823–1900), from Kreisburg, Lublin was one of the most influential thinkers and prolific authors in the history of the Chassidic movement. Born into a non-chassidic rabbinic family, Rabbi Tzadok became famous as a child prodigy authoring numerous articles and books, treasured by scholars everywhere. Later in life, Rabbi Tzadok became chassidic and a disciple of the Izbitcher Rabbi. Eventually, he was appointed the Rabbi of Lublin. Having excelled in both the chassidic and non-chassidic world, Rabbi Tzaddok's writings are a synthesis of analytical logic and mysticism. He wrote *Pri Tzaddik* (reflections on Torah and the festivals), *Resisei Laylah, Kedushat Shabbat, Machshevot Charutz, Dover Tzedek, Yisrael Kedoshim* and other works which became classics, their profound thoughts having an enormous impact. Referenced on pages 29, 35.

שפת אמת ***Sefat Emet*, Rabbi Yehudah Aryeh Leib Alter**, (1847–1905), from Góra Kalwaria (Ger), Poland was orphaned as a child and raised by his grandfather Rabbi Yitzchak Meir, the founding Rabbi of the Gerrer dynasty. After Rabbi Yitzchak's death in 1866, his *Chassidim* requested Rabbi Yehudah Aryeh Leib who was only eighteen years old to succeed him. He refused at first and only accepted to become the head (*admor*) of Gur four years later. In this position he wielded a wide influence and established the leadership of Gur *Chassidim* in Poland. A distinguished scholar, modest in behavior, Rabbi Yehudah Aryeh Leib won the confidence of rabbis and communal leaders throughout Jewry. He devoted much energy to promote Torah study and attracted many of the youth. His writings are collected under the title *Sefat Emet*, after which he is known. Its five sections on the Torah include addresses on Shabbat and festivals, distinguished by the profundity of their ideas, the clarity of exposition, and reflect the marked influence of the Maharal of Prague. Referenced on pages 16, 17, 51, 53, 54, 126.

רב יהודה מאיר שפירא Rabbi Yehudah Meir Shapira, (1887–1933), from Austria was a prominent chassidic rabbi, and great Torah scholar. He is noted for his founding of the *Daf Yomi* (the worldwide learning of a daily Talmud page) in 1923 and the establishment of the Chachmei Lublin Yeshiva in 1930. This was the first chassidic yeshiva in Poland, modeled after Lithuanian *yeshivot* such as the famous Volozhin Yeshiva. In addition, Rabbi Shapira held various other responsibilities including serving as head of the education department of *Agudat Yisrael* in East Galicia, becoming president of *Agudat Yisrael* in Poland in 1922, and later president of the rabbinical court in Lublin. Rabbi Shapira's two major works are *Ohr HaMeir* and *Imrei Da'at*. He died three days after having been appointed Chief Rabbi of Lotz. Referenced on page 71.

עטרת יהושע *Ateret Yehoshua*, Rabbi Moshe Aryeh Frund, (1894–1996), from Honiad, Hungary served as *Rosh Yeshiva* of Satmar. In 1994 the Nazis arrested him and his entire family and deported them to Auschwitz. After his wife and all of his nine children died by the hands of the Nazis, Rabbi Moshe moved to Jerusalem in 1951, where he became the Rabbi of the Satmar community. In 1979, he was elected *av beit din* of the *Edah HaChareidis*, a position which he fulfilled until his death. Referenced on page 24.

רבי מנחם מענדל שניאורסון Rabbi Menachem Mendel Schneerson, (1902–1994), from Ukraine settled in New York in 1941 and served as the Rabbi of the Lubavitch movement for forty-four years. While appearing to be an "old world" leader he was thoroughly knowledgeable about the modern world and reached out enthusiastically to society-at-large. He encouraged the pursuit of virtue, education, and unity, and also emphasized studying concepts regarding Mashiach. During Rabbi Schneerson's leadership, Lubavitch grew from a small movement to a worldwide community of two hundred thousand members. He established Lubavitch *sheluchim* (emissaries), and sent them out to build Chabad-Lubavitch centers everywhere. Today there are more than fourteen hundred Chabad-Lubavitch institutions in thirty-five countries on six continents. In Torah scholarship, Rabbi Schneerson is known for his scholarly analysis and chassidic thoughts on Rashi's Torah commentary. His lengthy addresses to his followers about the weekly Torah portion were transcribed and distributed widely. Later many of them were edited, distributed worldwide in small booklets, and finally compiled in the *Likkutei Sichot* set. Referenced on page 186.

Modern Torah Commentators

מעם לועז *Me'Am Lo'ez*, the 18th century Torah commentary was begun by Rabbi Ya'acov Culi from Spain in 1730. After being expelled he settled in Constantinople where the first volume of *Me'Am Lo'ez* was published. Following Rabbi Culi's death in 1732, several later writers used his unfinished manuscripts and completed the *Me'Am Lo'ez* on the *Chumash* in 1772. The commentary on the Prophets and Scriptures began almost a hundred years later and was completed by various writers in 1899. The aim of the *Me'Am Lo'ez* commentary was to reabsorb the masses that had strayed from Judaism in the wake of the Shabtai Tzvi heresy. Many of the Sephardic Jews at the time were ignorant of the Hebrew language, and without access to traditional literature, they gradually turned away from religious observance. Written in the Ladino vernacular, in an unpretentious, popular style, *Me'Am Lo'ez* made the main elements of Jewish life accessible to Jews who were unable to use the sources. It extracted ideas from every branch of rabbinical literature, and dealt with all aspects of Jewish life, history, ethics and philosophy. The easy, colloquial style of the work gives the *Me'Am Lo'ez* a conversational quality. No work designed to instruct the Jewish masses had ever proved so popular. Referenced on page 65.

מנחה בלולה ***Minchah Belulah*** **Rabbi Mordechai Gumpil**, 1797, Altoona. Referenced on pages 66, 75.

חתם סופר ***Chatam Sofer*****, Rabbi Moshe Schreiber**, (1762–1839), from Frankfurt am Main, Germany was the leader of the traditionalist response to the *Haskalah* movement. In response to those who stated that Judaism could change or evolve, the *Chatam Sofer* applied the motto, *Chadash asur min HaTorah* – all that is novel (in this case in religious practice) is forbidden by the Torah. As Rabbi of Pressburg, he maintained a strong Torah education, and his uncompromising opposition kept the reformers out of Pressburg. Rabbi Moshe Schreiber established the most influential yeshiva in Central Europe, the Pressburg Yeshiva, attended by more than five hundred pupils and producing hundreds of future leaders of Hungarian Jewry. His Torah *chidushim* (original insights) sparked a new style in rabbinic commentary and some editions of the Talmud contain his emendations and additions. Referenced on page 151.

מהרז"ו ***Maharzav*****, Rabbi Ze'ev Wolf ben Yisrael Isaar**, (d.1862), from Vilna, Lithuania, was one of the main commentators on the *Midrash Rabbah*. Referenced on page 39.

עץ יוסף ***Etz Yosef*****, Rabbi Chanoch Zundel of Bialostok**, (d. 1867), from Prussia, (Poland/Germany) devoted his life to writing commentaries on the Midrash and the *Ein Ya'acov*. He published two commentaries: *Etz Yosef* and *Anaf Yosef* which appear side by side in the *siddur*,

Otzar haTefilot and the *Ein Ya'acov*. In the commentary *Etz Yosef*, he strives to give the simple meaning of the text, whereas *Anaf Yosef* is largely homiletic. Rabbi Chanoch Zundel was possible a student of Rabbi Aryeh Leib Katzenelenbogen of Brisk. Referenced on page 59.

הכתב והקבלה ***HaKetav v'HaKabbalah*, Rabbi Ya'acov Tzvi Mecklenburg**, (1785–1865), from Germany was Rabbi of Koenigsburg, East Prussia from 1831–1865. His commentary on the Torah, *HaKetav v'HaKabbalah* was published in 1839 during the ascent of the *Haskalah* in the 19th century when East European Hebrew scholars rejected the Oral interpretation of the Torah. With impeccable attention to detail, Rabbi Mecklenburg demonstrates the absolute indivisibility of the Written and Oral Torah according to the correct understanding of Hebrew language. This influential Torah commentary demonstrates, *parashah* by *parashah*, how the written Torah without the Oral Torah is not only incomplete, but is against the Torah's moral and ethical principles. Referenced on page 107.

מלבי"ם ***Malbim*, Rabbi Meir Loeb ben Yechiel Michael**, (1809–1879), from Volhynia, Ukraine was the most prolific Torah exegete in modern time. He was appointed Rabbi of Wreschen (district of Posen) in 1839, and became the Chief Rabbi of Romania in 1858. Because of his uncompromising stand against the *Haskalah* movement, Malbim suffered much persecution and was forced to leave Romania in 1864. After having served as rabbi in Leczyca, Kherson, and Mogilev where he was likewise persecuted; he was invited to become Rabbi of Kremenchug, Poltava in 1879, but died in Kiev on his way there. Malbim's fame and immense popularity rests upon his widely esteemed commentary on the *Tanach*. This work strengthened the position of Torah Judaism in the spheres of exegesis, knowledge of Hebrew, and the exposition of the Torah according to its simple meaning (*peshat*). Based upon accurate, linguistic rules, Malbim's aim was to prove that the Oral Torah is necessary and implicit in the simple meaning of the verses and in the profundity of the language. Malbim's commentary on the Scroll of Esther was published in 1845; the remaining commentaries to the rest of the *Tanach* were completed in 1876. Referenced on pages 18, 28, 31, 58, 149, 150, 167, 182.

רב שמשון רפאל הירש Rabbi Shimshon Raphael Hirsch, (1808–1888), from Hamburg, Germany is the founder of the *Torah im Derech Eretz* (the integration of Torah with worldly involvement) approach which saved Torah Judaism from assimilation. In 1847, as the Chief Rabbi of Moravia and Austrian Silesia, Hirsch suffered not only the criticisms from adherents to the *Haskalah*, but also from the deeply traditional, who did not accept his more modern approach and emphasis on study of the entire *Tanach*, rather than the customary Talmud with selected Torah readings. His *Nineteen Letters on Judaism* made a profound impression on modern Jewish circles because of its innovative brilliant, intellectual presentation of Orthodox Judaism in classic German. It addresses the doubts and questions of those influenced by the Reform movement while providing insightful, penetrating answers. The *Hirsch Commentary on the Chumash* gained worldwide popularity for the scope of insight and information it offers to both the scholar and layman. Underlying the commentary is Hirsch's unique approach to the structure and etymology of the Hebrew language, with profound analysis of the letters and root words found in the Torah. Although Hirsch was possibly influenced by Rabbi Yehudah HaLevi and the Maharal of Prague, most of his ideas are original. Referenced on pages 15, 28, 55, 67, 72, 82, 91, 106, 107, 110, 112, 115, 120, 133, 147, 153, 157, 182.

רב ישראל מסלנט Rabbi Yisrael Salanter, (1810–1883), from Zagare, Lithuania the father of the *Mussar* movement established the first *mussar* society in Vilna in 1842. He settled in Salant, where he studied under Rabbi Yosef Zundel of Salant, himself a disciple of Rabbi Chayim Volozhin. *Mussar* literally means ethics. The *Mussar* movement emphasized refinement of character through the study and practice of Jewish moralistic and ethical teachings, such as *Mesilat Yesharim* (*The Path of the Just*) by Rabbi Moshe Chayim Luzzatto, which became the manual of the movement. The *Mussar* movement taught that talmudic study must be accompanied by ethical study and conduct and that religious Jews should be fully involved in the affairs of their community and refine their emotional and intellectual, qualities. With its new relevance and vitality, the *Mussar* movement rejuvenated traditional Judaism and attracted many Jews who otherwise may have left observant Judaism. Referenced on page 94.

רב שמחה זיזל זיב Rabbi Simcha Zissel Ziv, (1824–1898), from Kelm, Lithuania was one of the foremost students of Rabbi Yisrael Salanter and a primary figure in the *Mussar* movement. Rabbi Simcha Zissel's approach to *mussar* can be described as consisting of three principles: 1. One should become emotionally involved in his studies, whether joyful or sad, 2. One should ask oneself after learning, "What did I think before, and what do I know differently now?" 3. One's study should always delve beyond the external and arrive at the essence of the topic. He also taught that the whole world is a classroom where one can learn to improve one's character and increase one's belief in G-d. His commentary on the Torah, *Ohr Rashaz* incorporates these principles. Rabbi Simcha Zissel is also known as the *Alter of Kelm* (the Elder of Kelm) on account of his founding the Kelm Talmud Torah in 1862 to combat the Enlightening movement. A number of his students settled in Israel in 1892, opening *Beit HaMussar* in Jerusalem, under his auspices. Many of Rabbi Simcha Zissel's letters to his students were published in a two-volume work, *Chochmah U'Mussar.* Additional letters and transcriptions by his students were published as *Kitvei HaSabba M'Kelm*. Referenced on page 60.

חפץ חיים *Chafetz Chayim*, Rabbi Yisrael Meir Kagan HaKohen, (1838–1933), from Raduń Poland was an influential halachist and ethicist, whose works continue to be widely influential in Jewish life. His first book, *Chafetz Chayim* (1873), was followed by *Guard your Tongue* which organized and clarified the laws and ethics found in the Talmud regarding the importance to refrain from evil speech and gossip. He also authored the halachic masterpiece *Mishnah Berurah*, a commentary on the first section of the *Shulchan Aruch*, which is widely used as a reference and accepted as authoritative by Ashkenazi Jews. He was a modest and humble man who owned a household provisions shop, which his wife managed. In addition to spreading Torah through the world famous Chafetz Chayim Yeshiva which he founded in Raduń 1864, Rabbi Yisrael Meir was very active in Jewish causes. He traveled extensively to encourage the keeping of the *mitzvot* amongst Jews. Rabbi Yisrael Meir became one of the most influential rabbis during the late 19th and early 20th century, taking a central leadership role in the *Agudat Yisrael* movement in Eastern Europe. Referenced on pages 34, 37, 126, 130, 134, 169, 174.

משך חכמה *Meshech Chochmah*, Rabbi Meir Simcha of Dvinsk, (1843–1926), from Butrimonys, Lithuania was a prominent rabbi in Eastern Europe. He married and lived twenty-three years in Bialystok, Poland, before accepting the rabbinate of the *mitnagdim* (non-chassidic Jews) in the Latvian town of Dvinsk. Rabbi Meir Simcha is known for his writings on the Rambam's *Mishneh Torah*, titled *Ohr Samayach*. His approach is highly original, gathering material from the breadth of Torah scholarship to approach difficult contradictions in Rambam's main work of Jewish law. Rabbi Meir Simcha's foremost contribution is the *Meshech Chochmah* (the Price of Wisdom), *Meshech* is the acronym for Meir Simcha Kohen. This Torah commentary which often branches off into questions of Jewish philosophy was published by his pupil Menachem Mendel Zaks posthumously. He is often quoted as having predicted the Holocaust as a result of the assimilated Jews considering "…that Berlin is Jerusalem" (*Meshech Chochmah*, *Bechukotai* 772). Referenced on pages 22, 23.

רב אליהו כי־טוב Rabbi Eliyahu Kitov, (originally his name was Mokotow), (1912–1976), from Warsaw, Poland immigrated to Israel in 1936 where he helped establish the Union of *Agudat Yisrael* workers (*Po'alei Agudat Yisrael*). From 1954 he dedicated his life to writing and editing. His most famous work, *The Book of our Heritage*, explains the laws, customs and spiritual insights of the yearly cycle. He also wrote *Sefer HaParshiyot*, a ten-volume comprehensive commentary on the weekly Torah portion. It is mainly based on Midrash, Talmud, early

Torah commentaries, and chassidic texts, with many original insights blended into the text. Referenced on pages 31, 34, 151, 177.

רב אריה קפלן Rabbi Aryeh Kaplan, (1934–1983), from Bronx, New York was a noted kabbalist, author and translator with a background in both physics and Judaism. His close to fifty books are regarded as a significant factor in the growth of the *Ba'al Teshuvah* (the newly religious) movement. Rabbi Kaplan's works continue to attract a wide readership, and are studied by both novices as well as scholars due to his immense scholarship documented by his extensive footnotes. Rabbi Kaplan produced works on a wide range of topics such as prayer, Mashiach, Chassidism, Jewish marriage, mysticism and meditation. His introductory and background material contain much scholarly and original research. *The Living Torah*, Rabbi Kaplan's best known work is a widely used, scholarly, and user friendly translation of the Torah into English. It is noteworthy for its detailed index, well researched cross-references, and extensive footnotes with maps and diagrams. Rabbi Kaplan was also the primary translator of *The Torah Anthology*, the forty five-volume *Me'Am Lo'ez* into English. Referenced on pages 95, 96, 104, 110.

רב עדין שטיינזלץ (אבן ישראל) Rabbi Adin Steinsaltz/ Even Yisrael, *Shelita*, was born in Jerusalem in 1937, and is known for his popular commentary and translation of both the Babylonian and Jerusalem Talmuds into Hebrew, French, Russian and Spanish. Rabbi Steinsaltz is a noted scholar, philosopher, social critic, and world acclaimed author whose background also includes extensive scientific training. His classic kabbalistic work *The Thirteen Petalled Rose*, was published in eight languages. Rabbi Steinsaltz has authored some sixty books and hundreds of articles on subjects including Talmud, Jewish mysticism, Jewish philosophy, sociology, and historical biography. Referenced on page 5.

רב עזריאל טאובר Rabbi Ezriel Tauber, *Shelita*, was born in Czechoslovakia in 1938. He is a Holocaust survivor who immigrated to Monsey, New York. Rabbi Tauber, both a businessman and lecturer to Jews of all denominations, is sought after for his advice on practical as well as philosophical matters, often drawing on his vast store of personal stories and experience to convey his message. A former student of Rabbi Michoel Dov Weissmandel z"l, in Yeshiva of Nitra, Mt. Kisco, he has been the driving force behind many organizations dedicated to Jewish adult education and Torah dissemination. Rabbi Tauber is in great demand as a speaker lecturing to audiences from countries like Israel, Brussels, Moscow, Johannesburg and Bangkok. He has recorded over three thousand lectures and authored numerous books that have been translated into Hebrew. Referenced on pages 27, 154.

אמרי שפר ***Imrei Shefer*, Rabbi Shemuel Pinchasi**, *Shelita*, is the Rabbi of Yerushalayim's Machane Yehudah neighborhood. He is the founder and director of the esteemed and world renowned Yeshiva Darchei David and a worldwide halachic advisor and *dayan*. Imparting his vast and profound knowledge of the Torah, and the intricacies of Halachah, he teaches everyone from laymen to scholar. His widely popular *Imrei Shefer* is replete with original thoughts and ideas based on timeless Torah values and *mussar.* Referenced on page 165.

שערי אהרון ***Sha'arei Aharon*, Rabbi Yesha'ya Aharon Roter**, *Shelita*, author of an extensive anthology of commentaries on the Torah, published 1982 in B'nei Berak. Referenced on pages 62, 77, 100.

About the Author

Rebbetzin Chana Bracha Siegelbaum, a native of Denmark, is the founder and director of Midreshet B'erot Bat Ayin. She holds a Bachelor of Education in Bible and Jewish philosophy from Michlalah – Jerusalem College for Women, and a Masters of Art in Jewish history from Touro College. For more than two decades Rebbetzin Chana Bracha has taught Bible studies with special emphasis on women's issues in Israel and the United States. She creates curricula emphasizing women's spiritual empowerment through traditional Torah values. Rebbetzin Chana Bracha has a married son and two granddaughters and lives with her husband and younger son on the land of the Judean Hills, in Israel.

About the Artist

Carina Rock, hailing from Toronto, studied fine art at York University. She has been creating and teaching art for more than eight years. Carina studied in Midreshet B'erot Bat Ayin's part time program and is currently continuing her Torah studies in Jerusalem. She hopes to inspire young people in the Diaspora to connect to Judaism through art and creativity. Carina lives in Efrat, Israel with her husband, Baruch, and their two sons.

About Midreshet B'erot Bat Ayin: Holistic Torah Study for Women

Women at the Crossroads gives you a glimpse of the kind of Torah we learn at Midreshet B'erot Bat Ayin. Here we revive the Torah of our Mothers through holistic learning and living. We weave together Torah studies with creative spiritual expression, connecting with the Land of Israel, and healthy, organic lifestyles. If you enjoyed reading this book you may benefit from joining our learning program whether for a longer period of time or just for a visit.

Core Contents of the Program

In the heart of the Judean Hills, with its serene beauty, you will experience an approach to Judaism that bridges mind, body and soul. In the mornings, we immerse ourselves in authentic Torah learning of classical Jewish texts including *Tanach*, Chassidism, *tefilah* (prayer) and *emunah* (Jewish philosophy). During the afternoons, we engage in creative arts, meditative movement, gardening, and holistic health, including herbal workshops, natural cooking and nutrition. Nature hikes, community life, close interactions with Israeli families and volunteer projects are integral to the learning experience. The school houses an organic garden cultivating the special fruits of the Land of Israel; figs, pomegranates, dates, olives and grapes, in addition to a variety of other trees, vegetables, flowers and herbs.

Learning Style

Beginner and advanced levels are offered for women of all ages and religious backgrounds. Whether your interest in Judaism has recently been ignited, or you are seeking a wider perspective, Midreshet B'erot Bat Ayin offers the opportunity to improve your learning skills while strengthening your commitment to Judaism within the parameters of Halachah. The open-minded atmosphere at Midreshet B'erot Bat Ayin will allow you to discover the rich variety of Torah approaches while forming your own outlook and learning from the views of others. The learning program at Midreshet B'erot Bat Ayin will encourage and support you in the exploration of traditional sources with the aid of dynamic instructors, study partners and through independent study.

Beginner Program

Beginner students come with a love of learning and an openness to grow spiritually, but with minimal formal Jewish education. They learn to read and comprehend Torah texts in Hebrew, establish a foundation in Halachah (Jewish Law), and develop a deeper, more spiritual understanding of Judaism.

Advanced Program

Students with strong Hebrew skills and religious education come to Midreshet B'erot seeking a spiritual, natural and uniquely feminine approach to Torah study, allowing them to develop the vessels needed to create a personal connection with Hashem. Student-*Madrichot* learn in our advanced program while gaining leadership experience as mentors for our beginner students.

Conversion Program

Our conversion program under the supervision of the Chief Rabbinate's *beit din* for conversion in Jerusalem is for serious committed conversion candidates who have a minimum of one year previous connection with a Jewish community. The program includes full time learning, personal guidance, an adoptive family, volunteer opportunities and the experience of being part of a spiritual religious community in the heart of the Judean Hills.

The Village of Bat Ayin

The peaceful Jewish village of Bat Ayin, (Daughter of the Eye) is situated within the picturesque region of the Judean Hills. The town, consisting of approximately 130 families, is a model for joyously integrating the spirit of Judaism with daily life and traditional community living. Bat Ayin is populated with Torah scholars, movement therapists, meditation instructors, artists, musicians, nutritionists and holistic healers. The community is open, friendly, trusting, and safe. Midreshet B'erot Bat Ayin is designed as a micro-community within Bat Ayin where women of all ages and nationalities engage in intense Torah learning as part of an integrated, participatory approach to Torah living.

Bring Rebbetzin Chana Bracha to Your Community

Rebbetzin Chana Bracha Siegelbaum gives lectures across the world. If you are unable at this time to join our program in Israel you may be interested in bringing Rebbetzin Chana Bracha Siegelbaum as a guest-lecturer to your community. Contact Midreshet B'erot Bat Ayin at the phone number or email address below to book Rebbetzin Chana Bracha during her annual USA/Canada speaking tours.

Midreshet B'erot Bat Ayin:
Holistic Torah Study for Women
Village of Bat Ayin, Gush Etzion 90913
Phone: 972.2.993.4945 • Fax: 972.2.993.1215
Email: info@berotbatayin.org • Website: www.berotbatayin.org

Glossary

Abba (Daddy)
Akeret habayit (homemaker)
Aliyah (immigration)
Amidah (the central silent prayer – literally standing)
Avodah (work, worship or service)
Avodah zarah (idol-worship)

Ba'alei Teshuvah (those who return to become observant Jews)
Beit din (rabbinical court)
Beit Hamikdash (the Temple)
Binah/Binah yeterah (intuition/extra intuition)
Bracha/Brachot (blessing/blessings)

Chametz (bread, grains and leavened products not consumed on Pesach)
Chassidim (those who adhere to the Chassidic movement)
Chayot (animals)
Chidushim (original Torah insights)
Chodesh/Rosh Chodesh (new/Festival of the New Moon)
Chukim (statutes – a term used to describe mitzvot for which we have no rational explanation)
Chumash (Pentateuch)

Dayan (Rabbinic Judge)
Derash (homiletic interpretation between the lines)
Devekut (devotion)

Gematria (associations between words with equal numerical value)
Gemilut chassadim (bestowal of kindness)
Gilgul (reincarnation)

Hachnasat orchim (welcoming guests)
Hakhel (Jewish gathering at the Temple on Sukkot after every *shemittah* year)
Haskalah (the Enlightenment movement)
Histadlut (human effort)
Hitaruta d'letata (arousal from below)

Ima/Imainu (Mom/our mother)

Kohen/Kohanim/Kohen Gadol/Kehunah (priest/priests/High Priest/priesthood)
Kol Nidrei (prayer on Yom Kippur annulling all vows)
Korban (sacrifice)
Kos bracha (wine cup of blessing)

Lachem (to you)
Lechem (bread)

Ma'aser (tithes given to the *Kohen*)
Ma'ayan (natural spring)
Malchut (royalty)
Mechitzah (partition)
Mecholot (dances)
Melachot (creative works)
Menorah (candelabra)
Menuchat hanefesh (ease of mind)
Midrasha/midrashot (yeshiva for women singular/plural)
Mikdash me'at (a miniature sanctuary)
Milchemet Mitzvah (a war G-d commanded to wage)
Minchah (afternoon prayer)
Minyan (prayer quorum)
Mitzvah/Mitzvot (commandment/commandments)
Mizbeach (altar)
Mussar (ethics)

Nachat (spiritual pleasure)
Niddah (period of time from the onset of menstruation until immersion in the *mikvah*)

Parashah (weekly Torah portion)
Parnassah (livelihood)
Peshat (the literal meaning)
Posek (halachic authority)

Remez (allusion)
Reshimo (residue)
Ruach HaKodesh (Divine inspiration)

Sefirah/Sefirot (Divine Emanation/Divine Emanations)
Shalom/ Shalom Bayit (peace/peace between husband and wife)
Shamash (assistant/beadle)
Sharsheret (chain)
Shatnes (forbidden mixture of wool and linen)
She'erah (flesh of body)
Shelita (May he live long! Mentioned after naming a living Rabbi)
Shema (listen)
Shemittah (the Sabbatical year)
Shes v'argaman (fine white linen and purple [wool])
Shir (song)
Shiurim (Torah classes)
Sod (the mystical kabbalistic level)
Sotah (a woman suspected of infidelity)
Sukkah (booth in which Jews dwell during the Festival of Sukkot)

Taharah (purity)
Taharat hamishpachah (the laws of family purity)
Talit (prayer shawl)
Talmid chacham/talmidot chachamot (a male Torah scholar/ female Torah scholars)

Tanach (Bible)
Tefilah (prayer)
Tefillin (phylacteries)
Temimut (wholeheartedness/perfection)
Terumah (tithe given to the *Kohen*/donation)
Teshuvah (repentance)
Tikun/tikunim/tikun haolam (rectification/rectifications/rectifying the world)
Tumah (ritual impurity)
Tzaddik/tzaddikim (righteous person/righteous people)

Yeshiva/Yeshivot/Rosh Yeshiva
(institute for Torah Learning singular/plural/Dean of Yeshiva)
Yibum (Levirate marriage – the mitzvah for a man to marry the wife of his brother who passed away before having children)

Zehumah (spiritual impurity)

Index